I0795624

History & Guide

THE FRANCONIA GATEWAY

This book is dedicated to the memory of Niels F. Nielsen Jr., caretaker of the Old Man of the Mountain, promoter, friend, and all-around great man.

History & Guide

THE FRANCONIA GATEWAY

Bruce D. Heald, Ph.D.

Introduction by Dick Hamilton

ARCADIA PUBLISHING

ISBN 978-0-7385-1041-5

Published by Arcadia Publishing
Charleston, South Carolina

Printed in the United States of America

Library of Congress Catalog Card Number: 2002105253

For all general information contact Arcadia Publishing at:
Telephone 843-853-2070
Fax 843-853-0044
E-Mail sales@arcadiapublishing.com
For customer service and orders:
Toll-Free 1-888-313-2665

Visit us on the Internet at www.arcadiapublishing.com

Contents

From the Rim Trail on Cannon Mountain, two visitors look down the Pemigewasset Valley. The Rim Trail begins at the upper terminal of the aerial tramway.

Foreword

It has been said that the White Mountains of New Hampshire are the most written about mountain range in the world, except for the Alps. Although that may be true, the Franconia Gateway has not before been seen from the perspective that is offered here. This region of the White Mountain has a romance and history unlike that of any other part of northern New England, and Dr. Bruce D. Heald has captured it all.

This treatise traces the forces of change that came about as the explorers, settlers, and entrepreneurs arrived in this wild yet beautiful area. It makes clear the hardships and crises that befell the earliest residents as they struggled to establish a home site and a community. It follows the stripping of the forests by the lumber and logging barons. It notes the tourists who flocked to the area for its natural attractions, and the resulting development of inns and hotels catering to their every need.

Each of these activities and individuals had an impact on how the valley looks and functions today. As the forests were stripped and the rivers were fouled, residents and visitors rose up to save and preserve the scenic beauty and tranquility of the region. The White Mountain National Forest was established, and the region began its recovery. From the early 1800s, people from across the country flocked here to relax and enjoy the spectacle of the mountains and the clear streams that are fed from them. Already, the wonders of the Flume had become legendary and the rock hard image of the Old Man of the Mountain was serving as an inspiration to the artist, the poet, and the common man. Then came winter sports and the development of Loon Mountain and Waterville Valley as skiing meccas, transforming the region into a year-round destination.

Join with me as Dr. Heald guides us on an unforgettable journey with unparalleled views—up the Pemigewasset, Baker, and Mad Rivers, through the communities of Campton, Thornton, Waterville Valley, Woodstock, and Franconia—to discover the historical secrets (facts that even I did not know), hidden treasures, and exceptional people who have made the Franconia Gateway the wonderful place that it is today.

—Dick Hamilton

Acknowledgments

I would like to extend my appreciation to the following people and organizations that have helped make this publication possible: the Appalachian Mountain Club, Mr. and Mrs. Robert Bennett, the Boston & Maine Railroad Company, Frederick Bremer, W.R. Brown, Dr. Richard M. Chisholm, the Concord & Montreal Railroad, Justin Conrad, the New Hampshire Department of Resources and Economic Development, Jim Doherty, the Granite State Monthly, Jean Hallager, Stephen Hanson, Allen Hollis, Thomas Starr King, George Moses, the New Hampshire Highway Department, the New Hampshire Planning and Development Commission, the New Hampshire Recreation Division, Niels F. Nielsen Jr., Eleanor C. Parker, Karl Roenke (White Mountain National Forest), the Society for the Protection of New Hampshire Forests, Samuel Webber, the White Mountain Attractions, White Mountain Echo publication, and the White Mountain National Forest.

One
The Pemigewasset Valley

Of the several entranceways to the White Mountains, none is more romantic and majestic than the Franconia Gateway. For nearly two centuries, this thickly wooded and sylvan valley has attracted artists, writers, poets, and tourists. Secluded villages spotted with white houses lie outspread in the sun between enclosing mountains. On one side, the mountains rise smoothly; on the other, they bristle and storm the sky with their gray turrets. Over the broad meadows and intervales, shadows of oncoming clouds drift swiftly and noiselessly, turning the light on and then off. All the while, the winding Pemigewasset River—here dark and glossy, there white with foam—appears and disappears, finally becoming lost to view in the blended distance.

The Pemigewasset Valley has always been an important route through the mountains via Franconia Notch. As its Native American name implies, it is the "valley of the winding water among the mountain pines." Some 25 miles long, it is at its widest no more than 3 or 4 miles across. For most of its length, the valley runs straight and true, and its angle of ascent is gradual. In summer, it is a carpet of green, level as a floor, adorned with clumps of elms, groves of maples, and strips of rich, brown tilled soil.

At the foot of Franconia Notch, the Pemigewasset River suddenly bursts into sunlight and the world, dazzled. Shut in by mountain walls with high granite fronts in a country wild and picturesque almost beyond description, the river has scaled one of the most magnificent waterfalls in New England, run the gauntlet of the Flume gorge, flowed under the frown of the Old Man of the Mountain, and fringed the rim of Agassiz Basin—said by the Indians to be the bathing pool where the goddess of the mountains wed with the daughters of men.

The headwaters of the river is Profile Lake, formerly known as Ferrin's Pond and later as the Old Man's Washbowl, located at the foot of Cannon Mountain. Through most of its course, the river flows quietly on a fairly flat floor but, occasionally, as at Livermore Falls it plunges violently through a deep, narrow gorge. The other streams of the area, with the exception of a few small ones that flow into Squam Lake, are tributaries of the Pemigewasset River. Two of these tributaries are worthy of mention: the Baker River, which flows into the Pemigewasset from the west just north of Plymouth, and the Mad River, which flows through the northeast corner of the valley southwest into the Pemigewasset, entering the valley at the end of its 12-mile-long route, a rapid stream, coursing over a bed of broken rock. The Pemigewasset continues to flow in a southerly direction until it joins with the Winnipesaukee River at Franklin Fall. At their confluence the two rivers become the Merrimack River, which travels south through Concord and Manchester, on through the Massachusetts industrial cities of Lawrence, Lowell, and Haverhill, and finally into the Atlantic Ocean.

The means of travel through the valley has changed with the times. The Native Americans and, later, the pioneers came and went on foot. As transportation improved travelers used the horse and then the stagecoach, with its two, four, or six spirited horses. Next, it was the iron

Riding high in a stagecoach, early tourists pass along the stage route into the White Mountains for their summer vacation. This print of a wood engraving appeared in Harper's Weekly *on August 20, 1870.*

horse, with breath of smoke and heart of flame. For several years, the stagecoach and railroad vied for supremacy. Then, just as the contest was being decided, the automobile arrived.

Today, Franconia Notch State Park covers more than 6,000 acres on both sides of the Pemigewasset along an 8-mile stretch. The park includes waterfalls in greater numbers than any area of equal extent in the White Mountains. It boasts magnificent views from the Appalachian Trail over Mounts Lincoln and Lafayette, especially along the Knife Edge, an area of sheer-falling cliffs. Mount Tecumseh (4,004 feet), in the northeast part of Waterville Valley, is the highest peak. Jennings Peak (3,500 feet) and Sandwich Mountain (3,993 feet), lying near the eastern edge of the area, are the highest mountains in the western end of the Sandwich Range.

Geology

Geologists believe that approximately one million years ago, stream erosion was interrupted by the advance of a great sheet of ice that covered the eastern United States as far south as Long Island, New York. The sheet developed as a huge icecap centered in Labrador and slowly spread out in all directions, covering everything, even Mount Washington, the highest peak in New England. As it advanced, the ice scooped up soil, sand, gravel, boulders, and even great pieces of bedrock. These fragments embedded in the ice scratched and polished the rock surface and in many places smoothed and rounded the hills and mountains. The scratches, or glacial striae, are visible today on many rock ledges. As the climate became

5 — Present. Region was eroded to present topography.

The diagram illustrates the geology of the Plymouth quadrangle. The cross sections represent mile-deep trenches running from southwest on the left to northeast on the right. Each section shows a stage in the development of the region: dl, *Littleton formation;* kgm, *Kinsman quartz monzonite;* nqm, *Norway quartz monzonite;* co, *Concord granite;* mo, *Mount Osceola granite;* cg, *Conway granite.*

warmer, the ice melted, dropping the debris which it had gathered along its journey. This material, called glacial drift, now covers most of the bedrock in glaciated regions. Meltwater from the glaciers carried quantities of the small particles into temporary lakes, where they accumulated as beds of clay and sand. Some 30,000 years ago, the last of the ice melted away, and since that time there has been little change in the topography.

Valleys such as the Pemigewasset are more deeply etched out in areas where rock decays readily or where natural joint cracks make excavation more rapid. A broad lowland was developed in the Winnipesaukee district on weak granite and down the Connecticut Valley on minutely split slates. Conversely, mountains are left generally on the toughest rocks; metamorphic schist preserves the high Presidential and Moosilauke Ranges, and solid granite holds up the Sandwich and Franconia Ranges. Because rock structures in the Granite State are very irregular in their outlines, the mountains and ridges and valleys thus carved present a rather disorderly pattern.

High on the slopes of the Presidential, Franconia, Twin, and Moosilauke Ranges, there are spectacular glacial valleys with steep walls and broad floors. These valleys are headed with amphitheater-like walls, some 800 feet high, known as cirques. Such landforms are unique to mountains with glaciers, such as the Alps.

Glaciers

It is quite certain that these local glaciers existed prior to the coming of the great ice sheet in New Hampshire, because such extensive excavation must take far longer than the 10,000 to 20,000 years since the time of continental glaciation. There is some question as to whether these same mountain glaciers reoccupied the old glacial valleys as recently as 20,000 years ago. They were small ineffectual glaciers because only questionable local deposits remain in Tuckerman Ravine, in the Presidential Range, while the markings of the continental ice sheet remain in valleys untouched by local mountain glaciers.

At least 10 glaciers carved the ravines on the Presidential Range. Two or three glaciers enlarged the valleys southeast of Twin Mountain. Possibly two or three short glaciers occupied basins north and west of Mount Lafayette. One glacier widened Jobildunk Ravine on Mount Moosilauke. The sidewalls and headwalls were steepened to craggy cliffs, and the

Franconia Notch, at the northern end of the Pemigewasset Valley in the White Mountains, contains a wealth of natural treasures such as the Flume, the Pool, the Basin, and the Old Man of the Mountain.

floors were smoothed and rounded by the sandpapering action of rock fragments dragged down the valley under the stream of ice, century after century.

Glaciers might still creep back today were it not that summer temperatures average about 10 degrees Fahrenheit too warm. Very likely, precipitation was heavier and snow drifted more deeply when glaciers existed in New Hampshire. In this connection all White Mountain glacial valleys lie either east or north of wide ridge acres above 4,500 feet, but not one lies on the southwestern slopes. This suggests that snow drifted from the southwest or west, much as it does today. Those valleys with the broadest ridge areas to the south and west of them supported the longest glaciers. Furthermore, cirques (basins) developed fully 1,000 feet lower down on shaded northern slopes than on sun-warmed southern slopes.

The tilting land spilled the three large glacial lakes out at least 10,000 years ago, and streams with a regular but gentle gradient took over. Down the steep and narrow valleys of the White Mountains region, the last floods of meltwater left the boulder-paved channels that have become the river courses of today. One of the spectacular gorges excavated in this way is the Flume in Franconia Notch. The swift streams of this rugged area have cut continuous paths, leaving no ponds or lakes of late glacial origin except on or very near the heights of land in notches such as Crawford (Saco Lake), Franconia (Echo and Profile Lakes), and Kinsman (Beaver Pond) where dams of drift remain intact across flat valley floors. There are also those few small high lakes wholly surrounded by bedrock and sculptured out of more vulnerable spots of solid rock by the glacier.

This was the scene at Plymouth following the flooding of the Pemigewasset River in November 1927.

Floods

As in most of New England, floods in New Hampshire gather and discharge so irregularly as to seem almost haphazard. The concentration and discharge of floodwater is due largely to the terrain and the distribution or rate of rainfall. Measurements of precipitation at mountain stations in New Hampshire indicate that lateral deflection of air currents and updrafts among the mountains cause very uneven precipitation. Other factors are the amount of snow cover on the hills and mountains, and the distribution of forest and open country. Generally, mountaintops get the most rainfall: up to 60 or more inches per year as compared to 40 inches in lower areas. Runoff increases if the ground is frozen, forcing the water to go directly into rivers without soaking in, as happened in the November 1927 flood. In the flood of October 1869, the ground was already saturated by a previous storm and could not absorb any more water. The sudden thawing of snow, which stores up the winter's precipitation, concentrates runoff, making spring freshets the most common floods.

Runoff

The runoff moves at different rates and becomes concentrated at various points. Once the rainwater reaches definite channels, the flow becomes irregular: slow through the places in which the streams have dug down to ledges of bedrock and fast through those that have developed rapids, where the water tosses and foams. The streams afforded waterpower for innumerable sawmills, gristmills, and factories from the earliest settlements until the 1860s or 1870s.

The Pemigewasset River was a natural highway for Native American as they traveled from Plymouth north through Franconia Notch.

Today, most of the mills and waterwheels have fallen in ruins and been erased by severe floods. Only a few stone foundations and sluiceways survive. Upstream from the ledges and dams, a watercourse may wind in loops or meander across a plain of flood deposits. The broad intervales, one or two miles wide, afford enormous storage capacity for floodwater, which may spread over them as much as five or ten feet deep. The volume of river water flowing down the valley may be swelled to 100 or more times the normal discharge. These characteristics alone, on a river like the Merrimack, would cause floods to gather and move downstream at uneven speed.

Winding Waters
In the days when Native Americans roamed the region, this river, known then as Winding Waters, was a noted trail followed by hunters and warriors in their transit between the valley of the lower Merrimack and the beaver meadows of the north. The north branch of this river, like most mountain streams, is formed by two forks, its source being in the Moosilauke heights, from whence it flows through Warren, Wentworth, Rumney, and a section of Plymouth—a distance of 30 miles. The Pemigewasset branch of the Merrimack passes through, touches, or drains in part more than 30 towns, altogether an area of nearly

900 square miles. "Till rolling down its wooded banks between / A broad, clear mountain stream, the Merrimack was seen."

Native Americans considered the Pemigewasset not as the main fork of the Merrimack but rather as the mountain section of the River of Broken Waters. Its source is a small sheet of crystal water springing from the heart of the White Mountains, far up the slope of rocky ravines, sheer cliffs, towering peaks, and storm-wracked forest. Running around natural barriers strewn along its pathway, this mountain rivulet pursues its lonely course for a few miles before being joined by another mountain stream, also the outlet of a rock-bound lake. Now as one, this stream leaps and cascades and dashes around boulders, loiters in cool retreats, and receives tributaries that increase its volume to the point where it is dignified with the name of river.

Artifacts

Previous to the settlement of central New Hampshire, the Pemigewasset Indians had a village near the junction of the Winnipesaukee and Pemigewasset Rivers. (In later years the site of this village was made into a public park and, during that process, hundreds of artifacts were discovered, some of which resemble those used by the so-called Red Paint People of archaic times.) As their numbers were diminished by smallpox *c.* 1680, the Indians moved upriver to the intervales above Plymouth where there had been a village many years earlier. They were still known as the Pemigewasset tribe because their headquarters were still on the Pemigewasset River. Abbe Maurault, in his *Histoire des Abenakis,* calls it the *Riviere a la Graisse D'Our* (Bear's Grease River).

At the junction of the Baker and the Pemigewasset Rivers, on the fertile intervales by Livermore Falls, early settlers found the hills and ridges of old cornfields and the ashes of old campfires with arrowheads, stone mortars, pestles, and other implements. Black bears have always been numerous in the Pemigewasset Valley. (Thomas Locke, an early settler living near Danforth Brook in the town of Bristol from 1777 to 1782, killed 16 bears on Briar Hill.) The prevailing growths of oak and beech trees produced tons of acorns and beechnuts, which attracted bears, deer, raccoons, and passenger pigeons. Indians from Coos, Ossipee, Penacook, and Winnipesaukee came to hunt with the friendly Pemigewassets, who welcomed them with feasting and rollicking by young and old. Before the Native American tribes became reduced in numbers by pestilence and emigration, nearly 3,000 Indians lived along the banks of the Merrimack and its tributaries, from the White Mountains to the Atlantic, a distance of some 200 miles. By 1674, according to General Gookin in his *Historical Collections of the Indians*, "There are not of this people left at this day three hundred men besides women and children."

Richard A. Musgrove's *History of Bristol* mentions the many artifacts found at Newfound Lake near Whittemore's point and Fowler's River. The dam at the outlet of the lake raised the water level enough to cover practically all of the lakeside campsites. One of the favorite campsites of the Pemigewasset Indians was at Profile Falls on the Smith River, and another was at the spring near the old highway from Bristol to the town of Hill. At Bristol the Pemigewasset and Pass-aqua-nik trails joined with the Mascoma trail, which followed the Smith River in from Danbury and Lebanon. The Kancamagus trail joined the Pemigewasset trail at Woodstock, and the Asquamchumauke trail joined it at that tribe's old village site near the mouth of the Baker River just above Plymouth.

The Petition

In October 1743, an Indian named Coaus came to a council held in Portsmouth and petitioned the governor to place a truck house or trading post "near Pemigewasset where they might have such supplies as was necessary for their furs and that they might not be imposed on as they often were when they came into the lower towns and that they thought it reasonable to have some satisfaction for the lands if the English settled it, they never having

This view of the Pemigewasset River looks northward toward Franconia Notch.

had any as set."

The governor asked Coaus if the needs of his people might be met by having a suitable person at Canterbury to supply them, and Coaus said that would do very well. The governor then asked, "How many Indians are there?" Coaus replied, "There are but three or four that claim the lands at Pemigewasset." The governor also asked what things would be most suitable, and the reply was "Powder, shot, bullets, flints, knives, blankets, shirts, cloth for stockings, pipes, tobacco and rum." On being asked how many Indians would come down, Coaus said that there would be 15 and that they would come in the spring when the snow was gone. He further said that if the governor would send them word at Canterbury, they would give notice to the rest of the Indians and come "at his excellency's time." The governor told Coaus that the matter of a truck house would be brought up at the next meeting of the assembly.

The Response

On October 29, 1743, the New Hampshire House of Representatives met, and in answer to the message concerning the appointment of a truck master to trade with the Indians, the representatives unanimously resolved "That if they can have no voice in appointing a Truck Master they will not make any supply for that trade. Sent up."

In this territory, Native Americans fought against rival tribes for possession of the land only to be eventually driven out by the Europeans. They faced Capt. Thomas Baker and his men and then retreated. Here, in the spring of 1752, they surprised a four-man hunting party, taking Amos Eastman and John Stark prisoner and killing William Stinson; only William Stark escaped. On one of the foothills in this vicinity, they plainly displayed the Tree of the Dead, discovered by Robert Rogers, the two Stark brothers, friendly Indian Philip, and others—a signal of the approach of the French and Indian War.

This is a perspective on the vast Pemigewasset wilderness in the heart of the White Mountains, with Mount Carrigan in the distance.

There are many stories concerning the early settlements along the shores of the New Hampshire rivers, including the Pemigewasset. Mary A. Proctor's book ***Indians of the Winnipesaukee and Pemigewasset Valleys*** gives Baker's account of his attack on the Pemigewassets. The Pemigewasset River was a natural highway for the Native Americans as they traveled from the North Country to the coast. There was one particular trail extending through Franconia Notch to Plymouth, one which came down Baker River to Plymouth, where the two rivers united. From this point on, the journey was made by canoes to the head of the falls, where the "long carrying place" was—the longest in the region. Many war parties from the north came southward over this route to the early white settlements, made their sudden attacks, and returned with their captives. This was the route of the band of Indians who raided Stevenstown, probably taking captive the first white travelers to tread on the soil of Bristol.

Exploration

The first military expedition to this region for which some record exists was that of Thomas Baker. As a captive in 1709, Baker had traveled up the Connecticut River from his home in Northampton, Massachusetts, to Canada. In his "*History of Coos Country,*" C. Powers gives the following narrative of Baker's expedition after he escaped from captivity. Massachusetts sent Baker as the head of a company of 34 men to ferret out the Indians who had an encampment somewhere on the Pemigewasset.

Baker procured a friendly Indian guide who led them as far north as Plymouth. When Baker and his party arrived on these meadows, the guide advised them to be on their

From the summit of Mount Moosilauke, a Native American looks out over the land.

At the confluence of the Baker and Pemigewasset Rivers, Capt. Thomas Baker encounted a band of Native Americans. The Asquamchumauke River, just south of this location at the Ox Bow, was later renamed Baker River.

guard. They cautiously moved forward. When they had reached the south bank of the Asquamchumauke (now Baker River) at its junction with the Pemigewasset, they discovered Indians relaxing on the north bank. Baker and his men carefully chose their positions and opened fire on the Indians, which was as sudden to them as a clap of thunder. Many of the Indians were killed, but others escaped to warn their hunters.

Baker and his men lost no time in crossing the river to seek booty. They found a rich store of furs deposited in the bank of the river in holes dug horizontally, not unlike those of swallows' nests. Having destroyed the Indian's homes and captured their furs, Baker ordered a retreat. The Indians were soon in pursuit and reached the white warriors on the poplar plains in Bridgewater. A skirmish ensued and the Indians were repulsed with great loss of life.

Counterstrategy

At that point the friendly guide urged Baker and his men to retreat rapidly, as the Indians would certainly return for another attack. Accordingly, Baker moved on immediately and did not allow his men to stop to eat after the battle. By the time they reached New Chester, the men were exhausted from the march and lack of food. They declared they could go no farther without nourishment, saying that "they might as well fall by the tomahawk as by famine."

Baker's guide suggested some "Indian strategy." He recommended two steps: that each man build as many fires and make as many forked sticks for roasting pork as they could in a given time so that the Indians would think that there were as many soldiers as their were fires and forks. The men followed this advice and quickly established the encampment. Later, when the Indians came upon the camp with its numerous roasting sticks and fires still burning, they concluded that there were too many men to attack. Thus, Baker and his men were saved due to wise counsel.

Powers's diary of his expedition further recorded that on Wednesday, June 19, 1754, "we marched on our journey and carried across the 'long carry-place' on Pemigewasset river two miles northeast, which land hath a good soil, beech and maple, with a good quantity of large masts. From this place where we put in the canoes we steered, . . . up the river about a mile, and then northeast one and one-half miles, and north about six miles up the Sawhegenet falls."

The Legend of Moosilauke

Legend has it that the Great Spirit of the Pemigewassets made his home on Mount Moosilauke. In *The White Mountains* (1876), James R. Osgood states that "the Indian had a bold spirit who dared to climb the bald crest of the mountain. They heard him in the voices of the storm and the mighty torrent, and in the thunder that muttered in the dark gorges and rumbled low over the crests. They saw him in the rosy hue that kindled on the peaks in early morning, or in the sharp flash of the lightning that leaped from the murky clouds. To him they sacrificed. The first fruit of the chase, the early green maize, the golden salmon, the wild duck, the goose, and the partridge were their offerings."

Once, the sagamore, or chief, Waternomee, with a party of his men, followed the Asquamchumauke to its source, and "there they camped beside a beaver pond, where the beaver ***Tummunk*** had built houses. These they did not molest, but set out just as the sun rose to go over Moosilauke to the Quannecticut Valley." Not often did the Native Americans climb the mountain, but when they did, it was only to save time and distance. It was a difficult ascent for the moccasined feet to climb over the stones and through the hackmatacks, as they called the firs and spruces, but upon the bald mountain crest the way was easier. When they reached the summit, the heaven, *Kesuk*, was cloudless, and the view was unobstructed. It was a sight the like of which they had never seen before. Great mountains, *Wadchu,* were piled and scattered in a wild manner over the land, and silver lakes, *Spies,* were sparkling; bright rivers, *Sepoes*, were gleaming from the dense forest below.

As they sat upon the topmost peak, the wind was still and they could hear the moose bellowing in the gorges below, the wolf, *Muqoushim,* howling, and now and then the great eagle of the mountain, *Keneu*, screaming and hurtling through the air. A sense of reverence took possession of the men as they drank in the strange sights and wild primitive sounds, for they believed that the summit was the home of *Gitche Manito*, the Great Spirit. The untutored braves were filled with awe as they stood in the dwelling place of their God, afraid that the deity would be angry at the almost sacrilegious invasion.

As the sun, *Nepauz*, was dropping lower in the western sky, a light mist collected around the eastern peaks and, above all the river valleys in the west, clouds assembled. An assembly of showers soon hung over every valley; yet the heavens above them were clear and the setting sun was shinning brightly upon the vapors. The wind freshened and the great cloud—purple, gold, and crimson above and black as ink below—hurried from every quarter toward the summit of Moosilauke. Then the thunder, *Pahtuquohan,* began to bellow, and the lightning, *Ukkutshaumon*, leapt from cloud to cloud. Streams of blinding rays shot down to the hills beneath. Rain and hailstones, crashing upon the infinite thick woodland, sent up the roar of a hundred mountain torrents. "It is Gitche Manito coming to his home angry," muttered Waternomee, as he and his companions fled down the mountain to the shelter of the thick forest below.

Two
Plymouth

The approximate geographical center of New Hampshire, the confluence of the Pemigewasset and Baker Rivers, was the gathering place for the Abenaki Indians who traveled between Canada and the coast. Today, this place is Plymouth from which one long valley leads up to grand old Mount Moosilauke and another strays over broad meadows through narrow defiles and under frowning cliffs to the heart of the Franconias. Splendid scenic views—river and intervale, field and forest, hillside and mountaintop—can be seen from almost every point in the village. In earlier days of mountain travel, the town was a stagecoach stop and the center of extensive trade. However, it was the construction of the Boston, Concord, & Montreal Railroad in the 1850s that brought the town new life and importance and gave it the high position among the summer resorts of New Hampshire that it holds to this time.

The first recorded evidence of European settlers in Plymouth dates back to *c.* 1712, when Col. Samuel Partridge wrote from Hatfield, Massachusetts, to Gov. Joseph Dudley in Boston suggesting that an expedition of about 40 men be sent to Cossett (Coos). Capt. Thomas Baker, an adventurous soldier of Northampton, Massachusetts, was selected as commander of 32 men, who set out to explore Coos County. Baker and his men followed the course of the Connecticut River to Haverhill and, turning east to Warren Summit, proceeded down the Asquamchumauke River to Plymouth. Just above the junction of this river with the Pemigewasset, at what is now known as the Ox Bow, the expedition encountered Native Americans. A brief skirmish followed, without loss of life to the explorers.

On July 15, 1763, Plymouth was chartered as a town. Since its incorporation, Plymouth has grown steadily as a prosperous academic community. The notable Daniel Webster made his first plea before a jury here. Famous novelist Nathaniel Hawthorne often stopped here on his way to the White Mountains and, at the end of his live, spent his final days here.

The First Pemigewasset House
One of Plymouth's famous landmarks was the Pemigewasset House. The first of three hotels of this name was a tavern constructed during the 1760s by Col. David Webster. By the 1800s, Webster replaced this early tavern with a larger two-and-a-half-story wooden structure that was operated for many years under the name of Webster's Tavern. According to White Mountain historian Frederick W. Kilbourne, "Denison R. Burnam purchased the tavern in 1841, enlarged the structure and changing its name to *Pemigewasset House.*" By the 1850s, the hotel had been enlarged twice and could accommodate some 150 guests. By 1859, a 40-by-100-foot wing was added parallel to the Boston, Concord, & Montreal Railroad tracks. An early hotel advertisement stated that the hotel's dining room was "the largest of its kind in New Hampshire and intended to conveniently service travelers who could enter it directly from cars across a level platform." In 1862, the hotel was consumed by fire but was then immediately rebuilt on the same site.

Running alongside the Pemigewasset Hotel is the Boston, Concord, & Montreal Railroad. In 1850, the railroad was completed to Plymouth from Concord. In 1858, it leased the White Mountain Railroad, thus continuing the line from Plymouth to Littleton. To the north, along the shore of the Pemigewasset River, the Pemigewasset Valley Railroad continued a line from Plymouth through Campton, Thornton, and on to North Woodstock.

The Second Pemigewasset House

The second Pemigewasset House was built *c.* 1863 by John E. Lyon, president of the Boston, Concord, & Montreal Railroad. A large and imposing structure, with accommodations for several hundred guests, it made a commanding centerpiece for the village. Nathaniel Hawthorne spent his final days at the Pemigewasset House, with his friend Pres. Franklin Pierce at his bedside. Hawthorne died in Room 9 of the hotel on May 18, 1864.

An advertisement for the hotel in the 1902 *Tourists' Guide-Book for the State of New Hampshire,* contained the following: "Although this house does not close its doors during the winter season, it is especially equipped for catering to summer patronage, as it is located in the Pemigewasset Valley, within easy reach of famous fishing grounds and such noted resorts as the Flume and Profile Houses, North Woodstock, West Campton, Campton, etc. It is on the main highway of travel to the White Mountains by both rail and carriage, and is a favorite halting point for parties touring the region by team. Its rooms are large and sunny, and special attention is paid to its cuisine. Plymouth is a noted resort of itself, and many attractive points of interest can be found within a few miles of the Pemigewasset House."

The Third Pemigewasset House

In early 1909, the second Pemigewasset House burned. The third hotel with this name was built in 1912 above the village common on Highland Street where the Herbert H. Lamson Library of Plymouth State College stands today. This one, a rambling wood-framed complex,

The State Normal School c. 1875 was located on Main Street, some 70 yards east of the present Rounds Hall, which replaced it in 1892.

remained in service into the 1950s. Then, fire struck the place and its remains were removed from the hill in 1958. However, the Pemigewasset House left a legacy of being one of the fine grand hotels in the Pemigewasset Valley.

Plymouth State College

Plymouth State College had its beginning in the Holmes Plymouth Academy, which dates back to 1808. It became a pioneer institution for the training of teachers for the New Hampshire district schools. The academy took the name New Hampshire Normal School and, in 1871, the buildings were presented to state officials and the school officially opened with 80 students.

Originally, the entire west block from Main Street—on an elevation between Highland, Langdon, and School Streets—housed the Plymouth Normal School. Livermore Hall, on the east side of School Street, a hip-roofed brick structure topped by a large, square conning tower, was first occupied in 1891 and its clock first illuminated in 1913 on the occasion of the town's 150th anniversary. Across School Street, two Colonial Georgian-style dormitories, Mary Lyon Hall and Samuel Read Hall, were built.

Over the years, the school expanded and changed from an exclusively teacher-training institution to an accredited state college of the University System of New Hampshire. Today, it offers majors in liberal arts, business, and teacher education at the undergraduate and graduate levels. Its primary concern is the development of the individual, including the students' moral, social, and intellectual growth. The college measures its excellence,

Visitors examine the Hanging Boulder, 80 tons of overhanging granite, in the Polar Caves.

not by the quality of the students who enter its doors, but by the quality it adds to those who graduate.

Polar Caves.
Approximately five miles west of Plymouth is an attraction called the Polar Caves. These caves contain grim reminders of the Ice Age. Stupendous forces broke from the mountainside huge sections of rocks and sent them tumbling down to this location. These boulders of all shapes lie on one another in extraordinary positions, forming gloomy passages and cold caverns, which live up to their name.

At the close of the Ice Age, some 25,000 years ago, Hawk's Mountain was marked by the presence of a steep granite cliff. As the ice disappeared, frost action set to work, especially in the wide cracks of the cliff. Huge blocks of granite were forced loose and dislodged. The large spaces left behind by the rocks constitute the present caves.

Native Americans were the first to discover and use the caves. The caves are situated in a wooded park of approximately 100 acres at the base of Mount Hancock, which borders the Baker River. The Pemigewasset Indians had a sizable settlement on the river, which they

The granite formation called the Pyramid and Dog's Head was once an Indian council meeting place. Today, it is a feature of the Polar Caves.

called the Asquamchumauke. On the fertile intervales, they raised crops, hunted wildlife, and trapped otter and beaver. Then they crossed the river and used the caves as a safe meeting place during the time of war.

In 1922, the caves first became an object of interest to tourists. Edwin Collishaw, with his imagination and business sense, realized the potential of the site as an attraction to the White Mountains. Among its major features are the world's largest granite boulder (over 50 million pounds), a mysterious hanging bounder (80 tons of granite), ice that remains in the caves in July, and the cool interior on hot summer day. Collishaw named the site the Polar Caves for the rush of polar air currents that emerge from the icy caverns below, which have never seen the light of day.

Privately owned today, the caves are lighted and have steps and ladders enabling visitors to move through the maze. Guides are available to explain the cave's geological features. Various boulders have been given the name of what they resemble: animals, an Indian head, a Colonial dame, and other things. In one of the caves, a stone ax and numerous arrowheads have been found. That cave is called the Indian Council Chambers. Other caves are named Mohanned's Coffin and the Cave of Eternal Chills.

At Livermore Falls on the Pemigewasset River in Plymouth, the first white settlers found fertile land for farming and power for gristmills and sawmills.

Livermore Falls

North of Plymouth the Pemigewasset River has cut two deep channels through its craggy bed. One of these was dammed for the purpose of deepening the other. The resulting Livermore Falls is two miles above Plymouth. The feature of this fall is the deep water-worn chasm through which it plunges.

Beyond Plymouth the first landmark of any significance is Mount Prospect, which rises to the east in Holderness, on the opposite side of the valley. This mountain offers magnificent southeasterly views of Squam Lake and Lake Winnipesaukee and northerly views of the Franconia Mountains. Some 20 miles above Plymouth, the Pemigewasset River divides the valley, marking the way north.

This bird's-eye view of Plymouth was taken looking northward c. 1900. It shows the Pemigewasset River and the railroad to the right and the business district to the left of center.

For 40 miles the Pemigewasset River flows north of Plymouth.

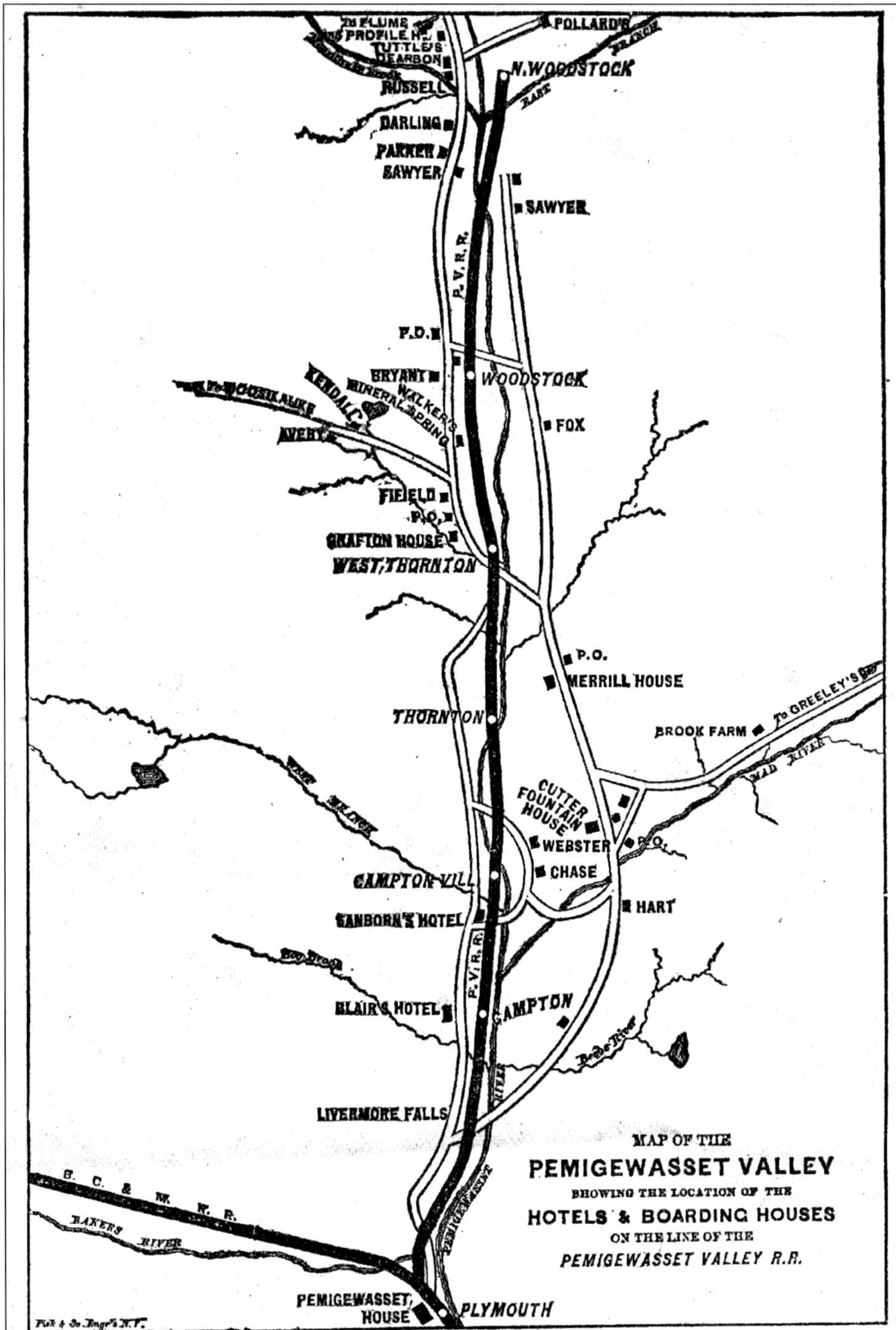

This map of the Pemigewasset Valley shows the locations of hotels and boardinghouses on the Pemigewasset Valley Railroad line.

Three
Campton

Some seven miles up the Pemigewasset Valley is Campton, which consists of four distinct villages, each several miles distant from the other. Half a mile below the village of West Campton, the road (Route 3) crosses the point of a hill that protrudes into the valley. At this point, the circlet of mountains encloses the valley on all sides like a gigantic palisade. However, to the north, a section of wall has been cut to its center. This is far-famed Franconia Notch. On the right are the clustered peaks of Mount Lafayette. On the left are the ledges of Cannon Mountain. The two great mountains stand exposed, though the lower and nearer summits of Mounts Liberty and Flume are blended with the higher ones by distance.

At West Campton, a row of maple trees lines the road and the renowned intervales appear as light places among the darker forested areas. Far across the level meadows, the hills of Rumney rise in smooth, firm curves. Where the clearings extend to the summits, the maple groves advance up the slopes in columns. Descending from the mountains of Waterville Valley is the deep trough of the Mad River Valley, and rising over the nearer elevation are the two blue-black peaks of Black Mountain. When viewed from the hillside pastures, these magnificent surroundings take on even greater breadth.

Some two miles up the Ellsworth Road from the valley of the East Branch, the massive Mount Hancock, with its one long, narrow scar, rises to the north, cutting off the view of Cannon Mountain. As the road draws near the towering wall of mountains, topped by the sharp peak of Mount Lafayette, the highway crosses the Pemigewasset and enters Campton Upper Village, on the shores of Campton Lake.

"Camped On"

Campton was granted, along with Rumney, in 1761, to Capt. Jarvis Spencer of East Haddam, Connecticut. It derived its name from the fact that the surveyors of the original grant "camped on" this place while running the original line. Campton was first settled in 1765 and incorporated in 1767. In the 1800s, Campton and West Campton were favorite spots for artists, who found many subjects of special beauty in the river, meadow, and mountain scenery. Even then, summer visitors came and, after the railroad system from Plymouth to Woodstock ran a branch into the locality, the yearly pilgrimage assumed far greater proportions, eventually outstripping other earlier known portions of the White Mountains. The visitors found that the area contained a concentration of all the natural characteristics suitable for camping, outing parties, and recreation, animated by plentiful streams, which for a while each year became violent torrents as the winter snows broke up and the spring rains arrived.

Although still a popular summer resorts, Campton today is largely a residential village. From Campton's Upper Village, the Waterville Valley Road follows the windings of the Mad River. The name long ago given to this stream is most appropriate; moved down from

Nestled in the valley along the shore of the Pemigewasset River is the secluded hamlet of Campton. This bird's-eye view dates from c. 1900.

the mountains, the large boulders in its bed and on its sides offer proof of the wildness of this stream during the spring runoff.

The Mad River Valley

Having dedicated one day to an exploration of the Mad River Valley, Jarvis Spencer found it to be one of the finest exhibitions of mountain scenery. The valley is 12 miles long and has at its end a rapid river, which courses over a bed of broken rocks. The Pemigewasset River is passed by a ford just deep enough to invest the journey with a short healthy walk. The ford has, however, been carefully marked by large stones placed at the edge of the submerged road.

Spencer forded the river and climbed the hill, which lies across the entrance to this landlocked valley. Right before him, sunning its three peaks 4,000 thousand feet above, was the prodigious mass of Black Mountain, stretching far up the valley to form an unbroken wall nearly 10 miles long, which apparently sealed off all access to the Sandwich Range. However, at the southern end this mountain, there is a slight break that allows passage to a rough and straggling road, 1,400 feet above sea level, leading southeast to Sandwich Centre and other Lakes Region towns. This pass has since become known as Sandwich Notch.

Campton Village lies along the slope opposite Black Mountain. Girdled with hills and bordered by meadows, it is so beautifully secluded that visitors to the Pemigewasset Valley pass and repass it hundreds of times without discovering the secret of its existence. Its houses, half hidden beneath groves of maple trees, bespeak a luxurious repose. It was here that the Black Mountain House, built in 1853, once welcomed and accommodated 100 guests at a time. Across from heavily forested Black Mountain is the immense whitish-yellow rock

Located in West Campton, the Maples was a summer inn with room for 30 guests.

called Welch Mountain. This mountain has only scanty vegetation creeping among its crevices and bare ledges that brilliantly reflect the sun. North of Campton, the valley still displays the white of an immense rockslide that occurred in 1869.

Inns

Besides the Black Mountain House, other local inns welcomed visitors during the warmer months. The Maples in West Campton had room for 30 guests. The Hillside House, one of the oldest inns in the state, was known for its fine food and pure water. With accommodations for 55, it was open from June to October. The Maplewood House, located on the Pemigewasset River one mile from the railroad station, was open from May to November. Advertised as "quiet and homelike," this inn had room for 20 guests and was connected to a large farm, which provided the fresh vegetables and fruit served in its dining room.

Larger inns included the Stag and Hounds (Sandorn's Inn), built *c.* 1820. Accommodating up to 80 guests, it was open from June to November. In the 1902 *Tourists' Guide-Book for the State of New Hampshire,* it was described as follows: "The Stag and Hounds is one of the clean hotels of New Hampshire; nice large room, single or en suite. Amusements are plenty, such as golf, tennis, croquet, boating, fishing, a good livery, music, dancing, etc. The artist or botanist, and those seeking rest and pleasure, will find this an attractive resort." This pleasant inn hosted many fine White Mountain and Hudson River school artists, including famous landscape painter Thomas Cole. The Sunset Hill House accommodated up to 60 guests and was open from June to November. It has a 200-foot-long, 10-foot-wide veranda along two of sides. The inn advertised "sixteen large rooms, arranged both single and en

The view looking east of the Pemigewasset from West Campton shows the Franconia Mountains, a long array of summits extending northward.

suite to accommodate families as well as an amusement hall for dancing, dark room for photographers, a bowling alley, tennis and croquet grounds, baseball and golf fields, acres of pine forests, a rustic summer house, and many quiet nooks in which to sling your hammock or enjoy a picnic. Good fishing and bathing in the Pemigewasset and Mad Rivers, near. First-class livery for many beautiful drives."

This early view, looking south in Campton, shows one of the first gristmills located in the Pemigewasset Valley.

Campton, with its rolling hills and broad meadows and winding river, became a favorite spot for local and professional artists. Mount Tripyramid is in the background of this 1910 scene.

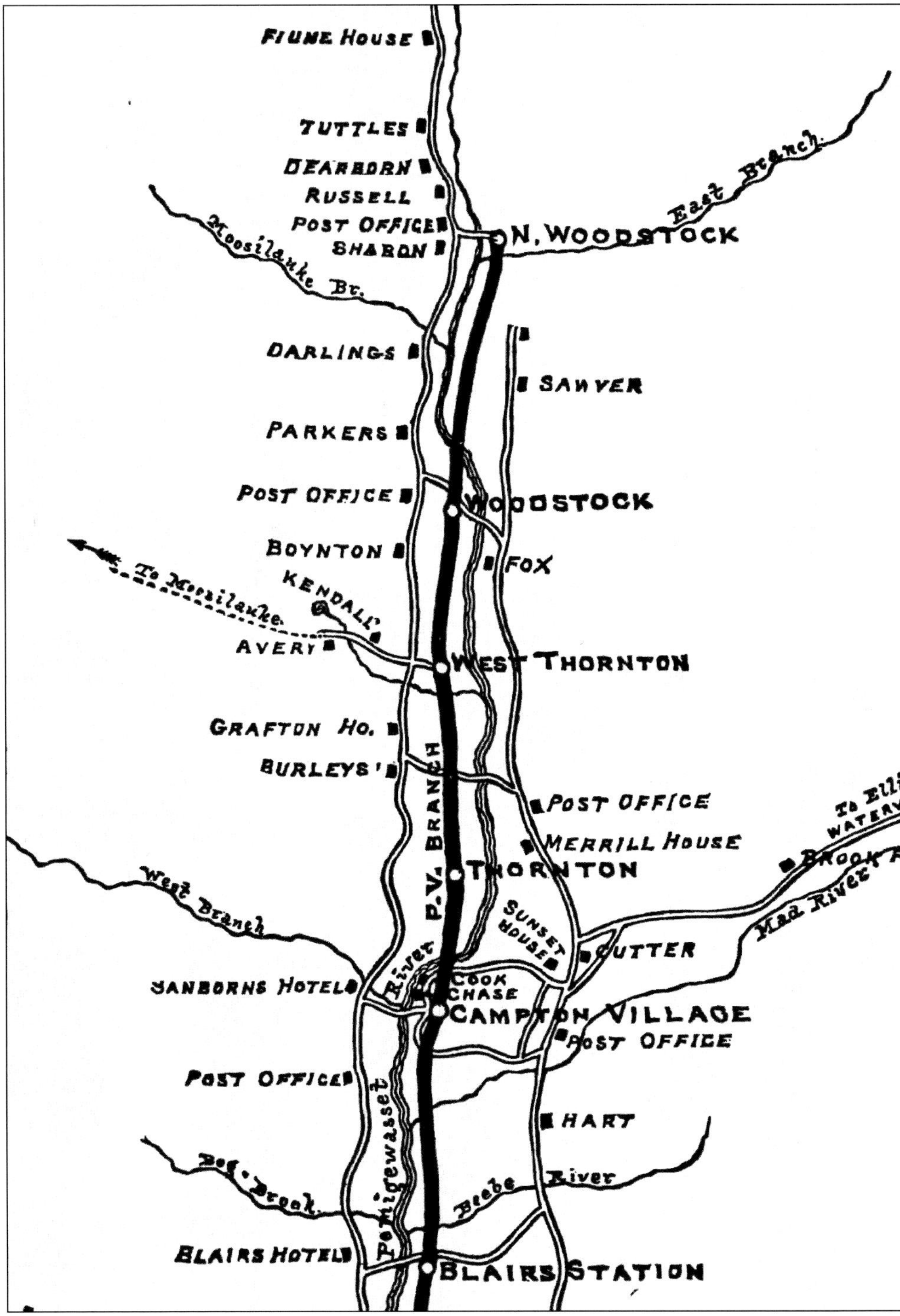

This map shows the Pemigewasset Valley from just below Campton to just above North Woodstock.

Four
Thornton

Farther up the Pemigewasset Valley, Thornton occupies a choice site. This pleasant town looks northward toward the Franconia Mountains. Thornton was granted in 1763 to a group that included brothers Matthew, James, and Andrew Thornton, and the town took the name of the brothers as its own. The first settlement, however, was made in 1760. Today, both Thornton and West Thornton, which is situated on the west bank of the Pemigewasset River, are made up largely of farms and summer residences typical of early New England homes.

Thornton Gore

Thornton Gore lies about halfway up the valley of the Pemigewasset east of Woodstock in the fertile Mad River Valley. In a sharp triangle of mountainsides, its majestic landscape is framed by Mounts Russell, Bread Tray, Osceola, Tecumseh, and Fisher. Clustered around this once bustling community are huge barns, testifying to the early productivity of these grassy slopes, and the ruins of mills, schoolhouses, and farm buildings of every description, indicating how desolate the region has become. History reports that the inhabitants discovered that they were becoming isolated from the outside world and, as the well-known restless longing for city life took hold of the younger generation, the farms ran down, the mills stopped, grass grew before the doors, and silence took the place of the busy life that had been.

A lumber speculator with a purpose of his own prompted and encouraged the desolation. George B. James, owner of the New Hampshire Land Company, bought up farm after farm. His policy was to let everything grow up to timber as fast as possible.

Logging

Across the breadth of New Hampshire's mountains, the drama of logging unfolded between 1875 and 1915 with the vigor and color of a Grade A crown fire. It was an era dominated by hard-driving, lusty lumber kings. It was a time of large fortunes made and some lost, of ruthless tree slaughter, of fires unequaled before or since, of grave concern and eventual opposition. It was a time that left deep scars, visible for many years to come.

Even today, the back country shows the telltale signs of this dramatic period: clearings in high flat meadows, signs of an old logging camp, and forest fire lines in the Rocky Branch, the Kilkenny, and the Pemigewasset areas. The logging roads on the sides of high ridges of Mounts Lafayette, Lincoln, Hancock, and Carrigan, as well as along the Bonds and many other slopes, are well-nigh indelibly etched. It was by logging railroads that the timber was taken from these hills. By 1870, the door to the forest riches of the White Mountains was open wide. According to the Chittenden Report of the U.S. Department of Forestry in 1904: "The policy of the state was to dispose of its public lands as fast as possible and large tracts were sold for almost nothing." The report continued: "The greater part of the White Mountain territory is a forest land, owned for the most part by large lumber and paper companies, and

Before the steam train made its debut in the White Mountains, logs were drawn from the forest by horse team, as seen on this old logging road in Thornton.

the timberlands are owned almost entirely by seven large companies. In recent decades the introduction of the steam locomotive as an . . . adjunct to the lumberman's logging outfit has increased the number of fires. The growth of the paper and wood pulp industry in New Hampshire . . . between 1890 and 1900 eclipsed that of any state in the Union. During this period the value of its product has multiplied nearly six times."

For the first 20 years, all locomotives were wood burners, consuming their own product on the premises. It is said that more than one engine crew got caught short and had to cut fuel as well as load it on the tender. Later, most of these engines were replaced by the more efficient and less incendiary coal burners. The earlier engines were four- and six-wheeled shifters with no lead trucks and, often, they were rentals or castoffs from the larger railroads. Later, as the derailment record piled up, different engines with lead trucks, smaller drivers, and other refinements were built for the special duties these operations required. The mortality rate was high on the early engines, and their lineage was often difficult to trace. A fortunate logging engine frequently was owned by a number of companies before it reached the scrap pile.

In general, the smaller logging lines constructed a very light roadbed, used a very light rail, and operated only during the winter months when nature had frozen everything. The larger logging lines, particularly those having long main lines with branches into side valleys, built a solid right of way on the main line and operated year-round. A number of these ran passenger extras consisting of flatcars with wooden benches. Several Appalachian Mountain Club excursions were organized on the lines out of Livermore, Lincoln, Swift River, and the Rocky Branch.

The major problem with these engines came not in hauling their trains but in braking the heavy loads on the downhill run to the mill. The only air brakes were on the engine, with individual hand brakes on the trucks for the brakemen to set up tighter on a whistle from the engineer. It was a unique operation, and no doubt many engineers offered prayers that their loads were not too long for the many short curves between the landings and home. When a hogger whistled for more brakes for the steep grade ahead, woe betide the brakeman who was less than careful going over the grinding, twisting log serpent, often wet or icy, in daylight or after dark. In an official report on the death of a long-train brakeman in 1900 the New Hampshire Railroad Commissioners stated: "for it is to be said that the business in which he is engaged is an extra hazardous one, that the machinery and methods in use in moving logs appear to be primitive and crude, and to afford little chance of even the most prudent brakeman to do the work in safety . . . we must expect similar casualties in which the best of men lose their lives." In fact, this kind of logging was life-threatening from start to finish, from the tree on the stump to the millpond.

A locomotive and its crew await the next trip down the mountain.

Hidden in the forest, this logging camp was one of many in the Pemigewasset Valley during the first half of the 20th century.

Milbrook Cascade breaks the silence of the Thornton wilderness as the water rushes down toward the Pemigewasset Valley.

The Woodstock and Thornton Gore Railroad (1909-1914)

For 10 years starting in 1907, the presence of the railroads brought the loggers. According to C. Francis Belcher's *Logging Railroads of the White Mountain,* "The Woodstock and Thornton Gore Railroad originated at a mammoth sawmill built by Thorne's Publishers Paper Company in 1906 on the banks of the Pemigewasset River at Woodstock. The logging rail line, incorporated and built in 1909, originally had as its destination that mysterious country to the east, Thornton Gore, or, as it was known locally, 'The Gore.' The entire tract was the property of George B. James and his New Hampshire Land Company. This area proved a clear stage for demonstrating how James and Company starved the life out of the farmers who once tilled the soil of this tight little valley."

The April 1, 1908 edition of the *Boston Transcript* reported the result of these operations: "Farther down the Woodstock Valley at Thornton Gore lumbering has been resumes. Here is one of those curious triangular bits of land peculiar to New Hampshire which have been named. 'The Gore' and here years ago there were extensive, old-fashioned lumbering operations. It is a beautiful valley, once given to farming, but now deserted, although the houses are in fairly good order. One peculiarity of the large number of companies is that they will not sell the farms, but hold them and let the buildings decay."

In 1907, all logging was performed by hauling the timber out of the forest to the nearby mills by teams of horses. By 1909, the Woodstock & Thornton Gore Railroad became incorporated. This short logging railroad line, seven miles long, made it much easier to transport the timber and, once again, the Boston & Maine Railroad took control. Belcher continues, "Once again the omnipresent Boston & Maine Railroad leased all the rails and track equipment, this time on the basis of 5% at $20.00 per ton valuation. . . . Combined rail and wood operations began late in 1909. Business was intense for only five years. At their zenith the two Woodstock companies had a payroll of about 300 persons, most of them at the mill. Timber cutting was done by contractors."

What ended the logging operations was, not a lack of timber, but rather the fear of fire. The Woodstock fire of 1913 actually became the beginning of the end for the Woodstock Lumber Company. The date of March 2, 1915, marked the official close of logging on this short railroad line—"the shortest of the White Mountain logging railroads," stated Belcher.

The old sawmill is no more. The bobbin mill and the big white house beside it, which stood by the shallow millpond on the Branch, burned not long ago. The big barns no longer hold the loads of fragrant hay that they did during the earlier days. What remains are deserted logging camps, abandoned sleds, cant dogs, landings, blacksmith shops, and other signs of the loggers' craft.

Farther up toward Franconia Notch, at the height of land between Mounts Osceola and Tecumseh, signs of the loggers' descent toward the Waterville Inn settlement remain, a disordered mass of leftover logs, sheds, dead shrubs, and forest debris scattered about as only a professional lumberman could throw them. Beyond the notch, other log roads descend, leading through raspberry bushes to the well-marked paths to Waterville Valley.

A Logging Camp

Waldo G. Browne, in *The Franconian Gateway* (1926), presents an early glimpse of the logging camp in Thornton Gore:

> After a brief stop at the lumber camp, we are off down the valley, past the familiar farm; past the watering trough, ever overflowing with the rushing profusion of clear liquid; past the oldest house in town, glancing at the stray herd of cows, grinding slowly up the long sandy hill. Here the birch tree view of the Franconia Mountains gladdens our vision, past the huge buildings that cover the idle mine on the old Mount Cilley Road, whisking around over the bridge in the poetic little glen to emerge by the prosaic town

> house and the long treeless cemetery above Woodstock village. Presently, we slide down the slope to the wilderness railroad tracks and through the confusion of freight cars, asthmatic locomotives, and scattered piles of lumber. Immediately, the old mill at the mouth of the Eastman Branch at the north end of "Foxville," gets scant notice as we wheel to the left and start away from Woodstock up into the back country of the Gore.
>
> Neat little farms and glimpses of the trout pools of the Branch are succeeded by overgrown pastures on either hand and increasing loneliness as the road climbs up among the trees. A small white school house on top of a hill excites wonder as to the source from which its pupils had come. A solitary boarding-house, with its chickens and vegetable garden, hints where one may certainly escape the fast pace of life.
>
> Our path now takes us down the hill toward the old center of the valley's life, passing an abandoned house and barn with relics of somebody's one horse shay in the foreground to emphasize the desolation. Down past more complete ruins, gaping cellars, and brambles over spreading the quindam door yards of thrifty citizens. The shade of scrawny apple trees next to a tiny cemetery, offer a place of rest. From this site a perfect vista of the valley below nestles peacefully against the strong background of receding terraces of hill and mountain toward the Blue Ridge. Sitting on a log in the notch between Osceola and Tecumseh, with shade of blest nature all about and upon us, it is easy to forget the busy haunts of men and yield of the nonce to the sweet fragrance of the out-of-doors, while an eager appetite attracts and empties lunch boxes in short order.
>
> Our day passes quickly. A rush is made through the tangled slash and under the wreck of an old windmill and the masses of raspberry bushes. Already, the shadows are lengthening on the sides of Osceola, and the recollection of the miles between us and the home fireside. One or two lonely axes are still swinging on Tecumseh's side, and the far away sound comes as an almost uncanny thing in this otherwise silent forest. Soon the dull thud of rolling logs at the landing, the tired workhorses standing by, the rough lumber men dexterously dropping the long stick into the desired places warn us that after all we are not far from the advance of man. We hasten our speed down into the village, there to be met with hot supper and good cheer, but leaving behind a memorable day in Thornton Gore.

The remainder of the Pemigewasset Valley route reveals more and more summits boldly emerging from the mass of mountains. Through Thornton and Woodstock, the spectacle continues almost without pause: at every mile mountains appear in new combinations. Gradually, the finely pointed peaks of the Lafayette group rise on one side and then suddenly pitch sharply down into the valley of the East Branch. On the other side is the high and mighty Mount Moosilauke ("Moosehillock").

This abandoned sawmill stands in the backwoods of Thornton Gore.

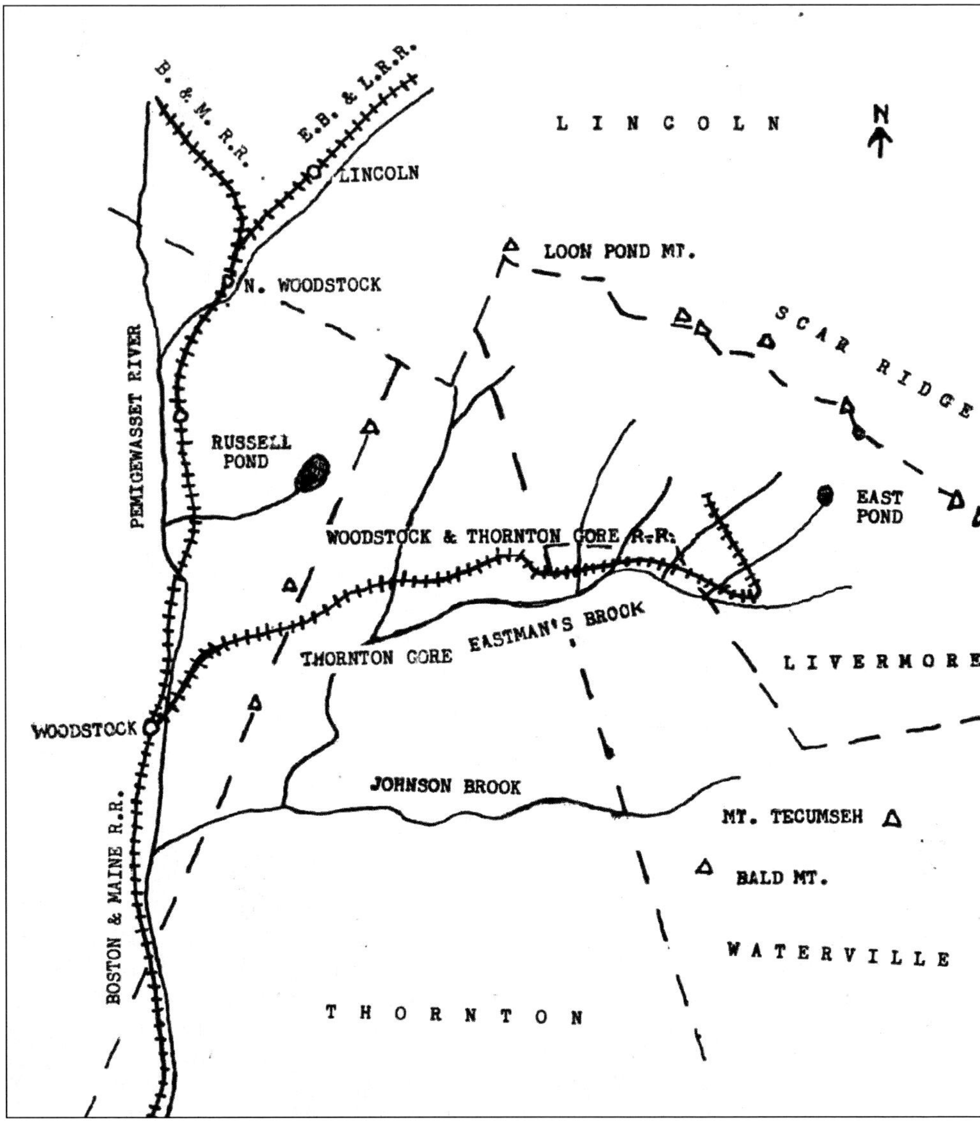

In 1909, the logging rail line was extended to the section of Thornton known as the Gore. In time, the Gore became the midpoint on the line, with the end of the tracks at Tripoli Road near the East Pond Trail. The entire tract was the property of George B. James and his New Hampshire Land Company.

Five
Waterville Valley

The wilderness in Waterville Valley was destined to be a favorite spot for the sportsman, angler, and lover of the old woods. It is crossed and recrossed by swift mountain streams; it is sown with lakes, glades, and glens; it is thickly set with mountains, among which the deer timidly browse and the bear and wildcat freely roam.

The Mad River drive is a spectacular journey with a bold array of features: rugged crags, furious torrents, a lonely cabin, high blue peaks, overhanging woods, and deep dense hollows. Some 18 miles from Plymouth and 12 miles from Campton Village, Waterville Valley has become a favorite resort for those who desire seclusion and fine mountain scenery. Encircled by mountains—among them Tecumseh (4,004 feet), Sandwich Dome (3,993 feet), Osceola (4,326 feet), Kancamagus (3,774 feet), and Tripyramid (north peak 4,140 feet, middle peak 4,110 feet, and south peak 4,080 feet)—Waterville Valley sits at the base of a great bowl. The town was granted to Josiah Gillis and Moses Foss Jr. in 1819 and was incorporated under its appropriate name 10 years later. In 1916, A.L. Goodrich wrote in *The Waterville Valley Guide*, "Seventeen poll taxes were assessed and twenty acres of improved land taxed, but the cold rocky soil of this high, northern valley offered few inducements for farming and by 1833 eleven of the seventeen men, two of the three horse, and four of the fourteen cows had disappeared." The first house, a farm, was built here in 1833 by Nathaniel Greeley. In it he entertained boarders, the first of whom was Ephraim W. Bull, producer of the Concord grape.

The Inn at Waterville
An inn was erected in Waterville in 1865. Surrounded by majestic Mounts Tecumseh and Osceola, the Tripyramids, and Sandwich Dome—all being over 4,000 feet in elevation—it was the only building in the township at that time. The inn first opened in Nathaniel Greeley's 1840s farmhouse, then known as the Little Red Cottage. According to *The Grand Resort Hotel, White Mountains* (1998), by Bryant F. Tollis Jr., the inn "operated for several years as 'Greeley's Summer Boarding House' and 'Greeley's Mountain House.'" Greeley then "transferred it to his son Merrill, who subsequently sold it in the fall of 1885 to Silas B. Elliott who then re-titled it Elliott's Hotel." In 1901–1902, a guesthouse called the Tecumseh Lodge was annexed to the hotel.

The following appeared in the 1902 *Tourists' Guide-Book for the State of New Hampshire*: "The Elliott's Hotel is an admirable testimonial to the enterprise of an energetic woman. Here, in a spot which simply excels in scenic beauty, Mrs. Elliott has reared an establishment and several handsome cottages to meet the taste of all summer sojourners. The many brooks in its vicinity are the joy of the fisherman, while the pedestrian will find no lack of mountains upon which to test his endurance. Wild and rugged are its environment, yet nature has succumbed to the inevitable and seen her domains opened up to the tourist. Rest and quietude can here be obtained in their full enjoyment, while at the same time there is no lack of entertainment and amusement for those desiring them."

This 1937 view was taken looking up the Mad River in Waterville Valley.

Over a 30-year period, the hotel was augmented by the addition of several cottages, and during this time, it became the centerpiece of the village. Not as imposing as the grand hotels, it reflected the design of some of the earlier White Mountains guest establishments, it provided first-class service and was large enough to accommodate 175 guests. The Waterville Inn, as it was called in its later years, burned to the ground on February 23, 1967. Today, Waterville Valley is a community composed of several inns and a four-seasons resort center, a favorite of skiing enthusiasts.

Depicted is the Waterville Valley ski area with its ski slopes and residential areas.

Shown is a junior freestyle competition at Valley Run in Waterville.

Landslides

During the past several years, interest in past avalanches and their catastrophic nature has revived. Landslides mark several slopes, namely the South Tripyramid slide of 1869, the slides of North and South Tripyramid in 1885, and the Cherry Mountain slide of 1885. The most famous landslide is the Willey slide of 1826, in which an entire family of seven and their two hired men were killed. This disaster prompted much study of landslides in general. More recently, foresters have strived for a more thorough understanding of the landslides in this region as a step toward avoiding deaths (two slides have claimed human lives) and damage to roads, railroads, trails, recreational facilities, and municipal water supplies.

The characteristic type of slide in the White Mountains has a long narrow track. It is what geologists call a debris avalanche. This type occurs on steep slopes in areas of humid climate and is almost invariably preceded by heavy rains; high water content is very common. The initial movement and progress on the steep upper parts is by slippage, sometimes on bedrock, sometimes with loose debris or soil. The movement then changes to a flow down the more gradual slopes below.

Early studies of slides, illustrated in aerial photographs (1954 series), were transferred by manual measurement to topographic quadrangle maps, thus locating over 500 landslides. Pertinent information on past slides, including specific dates of occurrence, lumbering and fire history of the area, and so forth, were accumulated from many sources.

Little exists in the way of descriptive accounts until the late 18th century. Jeremy Belknap, in his *History of New Hampshire* (1792), refers to the "birth" of New River, in Pinkham Notch, during a great freshet in October 1775. Subsequent investigation has indicated that this phenomenon was actually a change in course of the river flowing out of the Gulf of Slides, apparently caused by landslides in the gulf which brought down debris and dammed a lower section. During a subsequent freshet in 1826, the river broke back into its regular course.

Prof. Timothy Dwight traveled through Crawford Notch in 1797 and noted long narrow gullies where the precipices had been washed bare from mountaintop to base. In 1823, Farmer mentions the numerous "slips" visible on the mountains of the Franconia Notch area, stretching from near the summit to the base of the mountain. He also mentions two large gulfs in the north part of the town of Lincoln, made by "an extraordinary discharge of water from the clouds in 1774." It is possible that one of these was the Flume. There are also a number of references to the big slide that bared the south ledges of Whiteface Mountain in October 1920, for example, Jackson's account of Neal McCrillis who lived in Whiteface Intervale. These references are important in that they record slides which antedate the great storm of August 1826. From this date, many people became more landslide conscious, for on August 28, 1826 the family and hired men of Samuel Willey, nine people in all, were killed in the famous slide in Crawford Notch. The story of the Willey disaster has been told in print hundreds of time.

Many slides appear in a plate of the Presidential Range in William Oakes *Scenery of the White Mountains* (1848). Oakes believed that most of these occurred in the 1826 storm; however, he mentions the existence of several old ones on an uncertain date. "But since the settlement of the country, until the year of 1826, those of any extent or importance, if not absolutely unknown, were noticed by few persons, and feared by none."

As the country became developed, more people noticed the scars of old slides. Thus, there are references to slide scars in the Gulf of Slides (1879), in the Great Gulf (1882), on the col between the Twins (1883), on Scar Ridge (1877), on Mount Nancy (1886), on Mount Osceola (1883), on Zealand Ridge (1888), and on Mount Lowell (1874). Many of the more recent references include the dates of occurrence of specific slides.

On October 4, 1869, a heavy rainstorm was responsible for two large slides that attracted notice. One of these came down off Carter Dome into Nineteen-Mile Brook; quite likely it was in part responsible for the drowning of J.M. Thompson, the proprietor of the Glen House,

A landslide occurred on North Tripyramid in 1885. Note the man standing near the center.

Mount Tecumseh, seen in the summer from a cultivated area of the Pemigewasset Valley, becomes a first-class ski area in the winter.

who was swept away while trying to save his mill downstream on the Peabody River.

The Mount Flume slide of June 20, 1883, received attention because it roared down through the Flume, a famous tourist attraction, enlarging it a good deal and sweeping away the huge boulder that had hung suspended between its walls.

On July 10, 1885, the Cherry Mountain slide occurred, resulting in the White Mountain's second slide tragedy. This slide largely destroyed the farm of Oscar Stanley. Donald Walker was caught in the moving mass and fatally injured; he died four days later, on the day he was to have been married to one of the Stanley daughters. The base of the slide being near the railroad, a special "slide station" was set up and excursion trains brought thousands of sightseers to the site. This slide and the tragedy received considerable newspaper publicity.

August 13, 1885, was the occasion of another slide on the south peak of Tripyramid and of a new and very large one on the north peak.

The great storm of November 3–4, 1927, dumped heavy rain on New England and, according to authorities, produced the greatest flood damage this area had ever experienced. It came just over 100 years after the 1826 storm and, again, the precipitation occasioned a large number of slides. Among those that can be definitely ascribed to this storm are a large one in Pinkham Notch, at least four in Cascade Ravine (where J. Rayner Edmunds's Cascade Camp was swept away), as many as eight in Castle Ravine, the Cider Brook slide, one on Lion Head in Tuckerman Ravine, one in King Ravine, and three on Mount Hight. Several of those in Cascade and Castle Ravines were quite small.

In September 1938, the most destructive single hurricane of record hit New England. Heavy rains, falling on already saturated ground and combined with high winds, produced floods, tremendous blowdowns, and at least 13 landslides. Among these were the ones

Mount Welch (2,605 feet) is a spur of the Tecumseh Mountain Range. This view of the mountainside, taken from Mount Dickey (2,734), shows the results of the clear-cutting that was done during the first half of the 20th century.

crossing the Daniel Webster Scout Train on Mount Madison, several in Franconia Notch, two on Mount Passaconaway, and a number in the Ammonoosuc and Burt Ravines on Mount Washington.

On June 14, 1948, heavy but more localized rainfall caused two large slides that came down within 20 minutes of each other in Franconia Notch, cutting off road travel. Fortunately, the more northern of these, which was headed toward the Profile Gift Shop, barely reached the road; had it continued another 200 yards, it might well have had tragic consequences, as people were in the gift shop at the time.

Hurricane Carol struck northern New England on August 31, 1954, accompanied by the heavy rainfall typical of tropical storms. This was the occasion of the Gale River slide, which damaged the Littleton reservoir. The large slides on the south side of Mount Osceola and at least three more on the north side, as well as the large King Ravine slide, all occurred during this storm.

It is interesting to note that all slides for which dates are available occurred in connection with heavy rain. Large numbers have occurred during heavy general storms, especially those of the tropical hurricane type, but there have been a number of occasions on which more localized rains of summer thunderstorms have been involved. All slides dated at least to the month have occurred in the period of June to November. No records exist of any occurring in the months of snowmelt and spring rains, March to May. With one exception, all November landslides are attributable to a single storm that occurred very early in the month, the one on November 3–4, 1927.

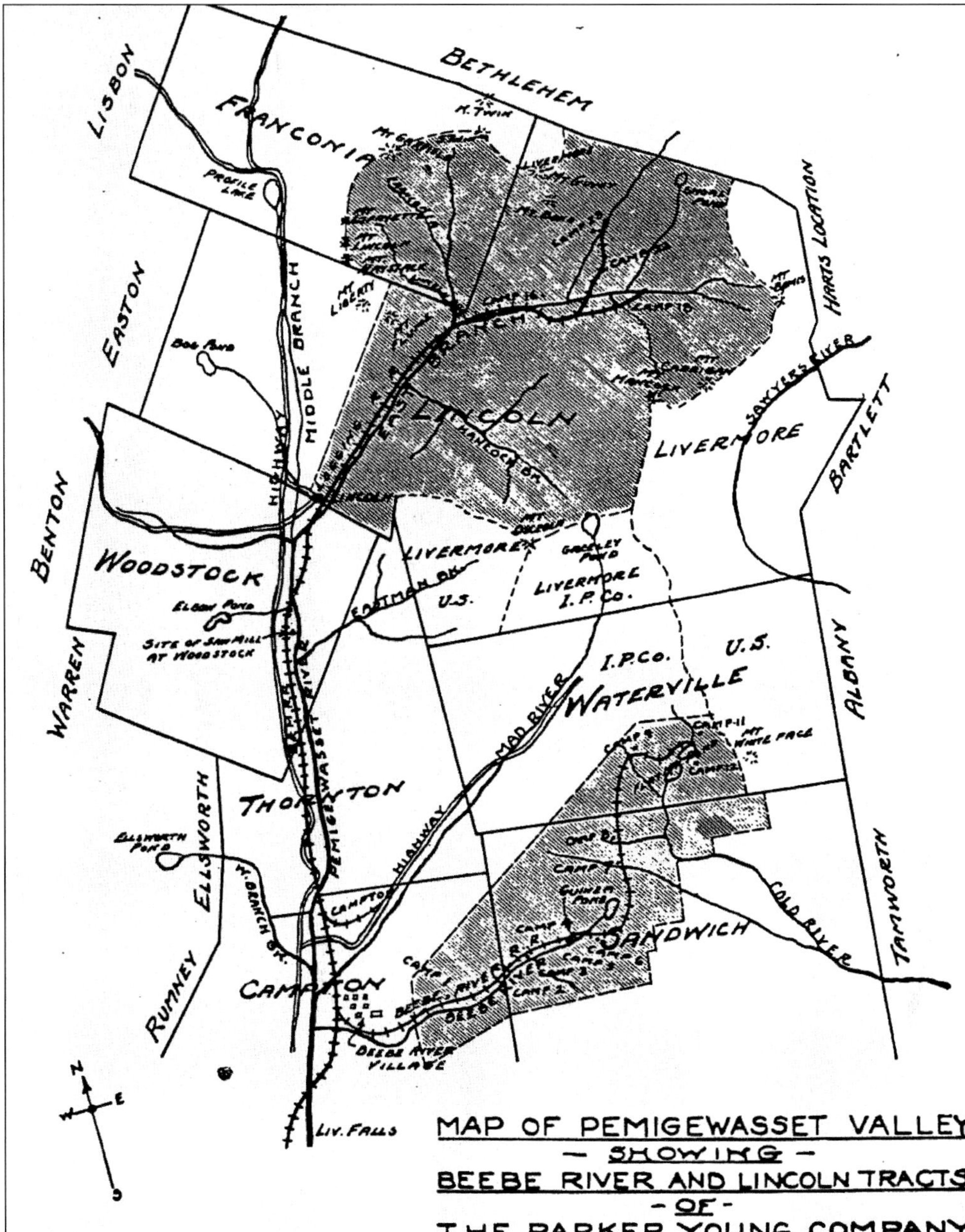

This April 1925 map of the Pemigewasset Valley shows the Beebe River and the Lincoln tracks of the Parker Young Company.

The logging crew and the locomotive pause for a moment on the Beebe River Railroad line.

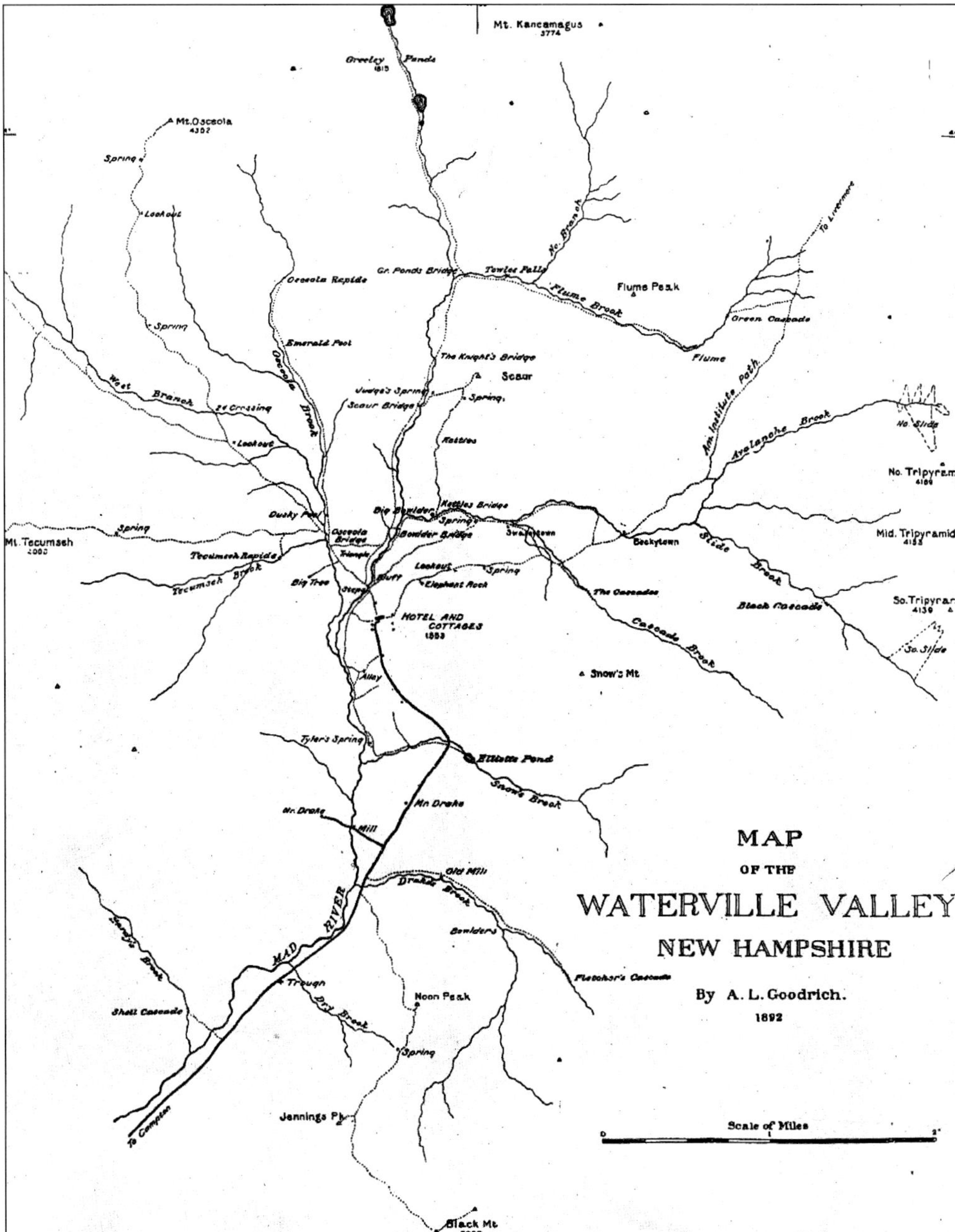

This 1892 map of Waterville Valley includes mill locations on the Mad River and on other local waterways.

This is Logging Camp No. 5, the Cutting Mill in Waterville. It was located at the junction of Mad River and Flume Brook on Skid Road.

Lumbering

When the railroad arrived, loggers came to the mountain slopes of Waterville Valley, resulting in changes to the climate and the clientele of the once farmland area. Large-scale logging operations commenced during the 1880s under companies and landholders such as the White Mountain Paper Company, the Publishers Paper Company, the International Paper Company, and, soon, the Parker Young Company. During this period the logging industry depended primarily on the waterways of the Pemigewasset and Mad Rivers.

According to the White Mountain National Forest's Waterville Unit Plan (1978), "There were more lumbermen than agriculturists, and many farmers had their own sawmills, relying heavily on logging and lumbering to survive on their rocky lands. . . . Starting about 1850, as the farms were being abandoned for the richer farmlands of the Midwest, forest lands in the Valley were bought up in very large tracts by land companies and trusts such as the Merrimack River Lumber Company and the New Hampshire Land Company. Extensive logging operations started about 1880 and continued for fifty years."

The report states that by the 1890s, "an extensive network of logging railroads was built in Thornton Gore. The present Tripoli Road runs close to the main railroad grade there. Sawmills were located in Lincoln, Woodstock, and Beebe River. Many of the old road beds developed into the current trail system . . . Most of this logging was for spruce, which was stored in piles below the driving dams in the winter and then driven down during the spring run-off . . . As late as 1915, the best spruce was picked out for ship spars. The rest went for lumber or pulpwood. The early lumberjacks and rivermen were a special breed, for they lived in the forests and on the rivers of the North Country. They were a product of the time and their environment, but now this has passed and they no longer exist."

Francis C. Belcher, in his *Logging Railroads of the White Mountains* (1980), wrote, "Official State and Federal Government reports show that lumber production in New Hampshire trebled from the late 1860s to 1900, finally reaching an all-time high of 650 million board feet in 1907. But the production then dwindled rapidly and never again challenged the records set in 1895 to 1907."

The Loggers

Grace H. Bean's *The Town at the End of the Road (A History of Waterville Valley)* (1960) comments on the life of the logger, saying, "From the 1880s up to 1930, the life of the lumberjacks was rough, dangerous, often spectacular, requiring skill and physical hardiness. The log drives down the river, for example, with their excitement, confusion, and noise, are unforgettable. Individual drama, too, gave an edge to the logger's daily life which sometimes ended in tragedy, sometimes made buddies out of strangers."

Since there were no roads suitable for transporting the logs to the mills, the only reasonable way to get the logs out of the dense forests was by water. As the early cowboy drove his cattle, so the riverman or "river hog" drove the logs, as soon as the melting snows had swelled the streams. River hogs began their training at a young age. Beginning at age eight, boys began practicing with the pike pole and the peavey, working first in the still waters of the millponds and later on the log drive. They developed an inarticulate love and respect for the river. The work was hard and dangerous; the food was not the best; the wages were very low; yet, the call of the river drew them, just as the open prairie drew the frontier cowboys.

The river hogs guided (drove) the logs from the rollways alongside the streams, where lumberjacks had piled them during the winter months, to the sawmills downriver. The drive sometimes took three weeks and sometimes as long as two years if the water was low and the logs became stranded on dry ledges. A riverman spent most of his time lugging and prying, lifting the heavy, inert timbers from where they were jammed against the bank and shoving them out into the moving water.

Log driving required special skills—not just the ability to stand on a log and ride it without falling off. Riding a log in quiet water and riding it in fast water required two different sets of muscles and reflexes. A trip in quiet water was often a relatively simple task: the driver stepped onto a log, stuck his peavey into it, leaned on the handle, and let the river's current do the work. In rough water, however, the driver used the peavey as a balancing pole and, if another log came rolling his under, he stepped onto the new log and continued his ride. Quick judgment, endurance, physical strength, and balance constituted the essential skills for a successful river hog. One other quality was highly prized: log sense. It came with experience, and to some more than to others. It included knowing the tendencies of currents, the effect of the water's volume and swiftness, and the places where jams were likely to occur; it also involved avoiding and breaking pileups, locating the key log, rollway breaking, and dam running. All of these skills marked the river hog who rose to the top of his profession.

When the railroads arrived in the 1840s, they opened up a vast new territory for lumbering, primarily in the wilderness of the Pemigewasset Valley. In the rush, careless methods of cutting led to the removal of large portions of the virgin timber. Valuable conifers—spruce, white pine, hemlock, and balsam—of which the primeval forest was mainly composed, were taken, changing the general character of the region. Evidence of widespread cutting remains, along with marks of repeated burning. In the early days of clearcut logging, tops and trimmings were simply left where they fell.

Until 1867, the state of New Hampshire owned the greater part of the White Mountain region but operated under the policy of disposing of its public lands as quickly as possible. Thus, large tracts were sold for almost nothing. The new owners of this rich domain were

River hogs log on the East Branch of the Pemigewasset River.

speculators who quickly cut great quantities of mature timber in order to pay the taxes and to obtain as much profit as possible. Every valuable timber area was either bought by or subject by contract to cutting by the large lumber and paper companies. At length, the increasing scarcity of spruce timber and the tariff on building materials impelled the owners to cut trees below the line of their maturity. This destructive cutting was reinforced by the demands of the wood pulp industry, leading some owners to clearcut entire areas, especially on high slopes and other places where logging was most difficult. In many cases, a quarter of a century or more was required to restore the forest; in other cases, fires ran over these area, consuming all vegetation.

New Hampshire's Mountain Forests

Ye mountains of New Hampshire, her glory and her crown,
Whose rocky summits proudly rise above the tempests' frown,
Around your shoulders, broad and strong, the ancient forest grow,
While from each cliff, with joyful song, the sparkling waters flow.

O statesman! spare the forests which grace our native land!
Save some of nature's handicraft from lucre's grasping hand,
That when your earthly labors o're, beneath their shade you rest,
The generations yet unborn may rise and call you blessed.

—*Samuel Webber*

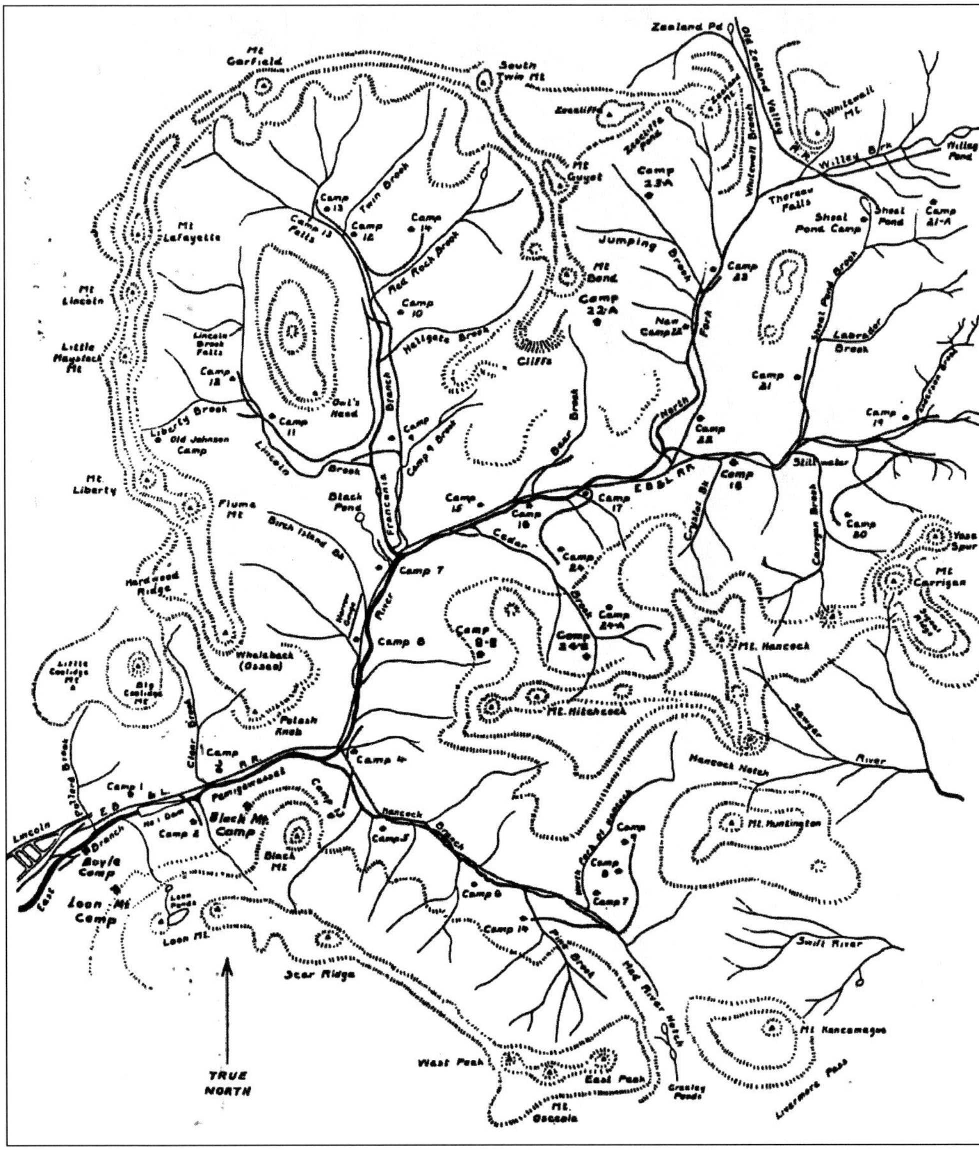

This map, prepared for a June 26, 1960 meeting concerning the Kancamagus Highway, shows the sites of logging camps and railroads in the Pemigewasset wilderness.

Six
Woodstock

The town of Woodstock had two other names before the current one was adopted. In 1773, when Gov. Benning Wentworth presented to Eli Demerit and 97 others the first charter of some 25,000 acres of land, the official name on the charter was Peeling. In 1771, the town was regranted to another group and was renamed Fairfield. Later, in 1773, it was granted back to some of the original proprietors, again as Peeling. In 1799, the town was officially incorporated. Finally, in 1840, the present name of Woodstock was adopted.

Referring to the early development of the town, resident Eleanor C. Parker said, "Since so much of the land is sloping, the first cleared farms were mainly along the Pemigewasset River. As the town grew, small mills, to provide needed materials, were built on most of the twenty-five streams within its border. By 1854 there were fifteen mills including lumber, grist, and textile. In addition to the farms and mills, people also found work at the starch factory on Eastman Brook, a tannery at Mirror Lake, and a lead mine on Mount Cilley."

North Woodstock

By 1870, the town had become divided into two definite settlements, northern and southern. North Woodstock was a summer resort, and Woodstock (Lower Village) was still rural and residential. After the Civil War, well-to-do people who lived in the cities arrived by Concord coach to see the pristine location and panoramic views widely celebrated by writers and artists such as Nathaniel Hawthorne, Henry David Thoreau, and Thomas Cole.

North Woodstock—located within reach of the natural wonders known as the Lost River, Indian Head, the Flume, the numerous waterfalls and cascades of Franconia Notch, Echo and Profile Lakes, and the Old Man of the Mountain—became a favorite haven for visitors, whose numbers increased by the thousands after the railroad replaced the stagecoach.

Accommodations

To meet the demand for accommodations, hotels such as the Russell House, Three Rivers House (Mount Adams Inn), the Fairview House, Deer Park Hotel, the Alpine; Dearborn House, French's Hotel, and the Mountain View opened in town. From the 1880s to the 1890s, North Woodstock was known as the "village of hotels," and many visitors came and stayed for the entire summer.

The Mount Liberty was built *c.* the 1880s to accommodate 30 guests, and was open from June to October. Situated on a plateau, the Mount Liberty advertised "A breeze of fresh air is always noticeable from this observatory, which makes it pleasant on sultry day. From the broad verandahs a sweeping view of the surrounding valley is had, which is especially attractive at sunset when the sun casts its golden rays on the mountain peaks." Those mountain peaks included Mount Liberty to the north and east; Mounts Lincoln, Haystack, and Lafayette farther to the north; and Mount Pemigewasset to the northwest.

The Fairview Hotel was open from June to October and accommodated 100 guests. Pictured in August 1922, the Fairview was a popular resort, known for its spacious rooms and attention to comfort.

The Fairview Hotel offered an excellent northward view of the Franconia Range.

Open from June to October, the Deer Park Hotel had room for 250 guests. This imposing L-shaped resort attracted thousands of visitors.

The Fairview

The Fairview was built in 1881–1884 and was furnished with special attention to comfort. The 1902 *Tourists' Guide-Book for the State of New Hampshire* contained the following information about the Fairview: "The sleeping apartments are light and airy, nearly all have clothes presses, and the beds are all provided with the best hair mattresses. The parlors are large and pleasant, and from the piazzas, which extend 175 feet around the house, grant and extensive views are had. We do not aim to give great style and splendor, as our prices, $6. to $10. per week, will not admit of it, but we do aim to give pleasure and comfort. The table is provided with the best of milk, eggs, and vegetables direct from the farm connected with the house, and the kitchen is presided over by one of the best cooks in the mountains. Excellent fishing abounds in all the brooks and streams near the Fairview House, and many handsome baskets of trout are brought in during the summer by guests of the house. Late stayers will find themselves in the paradise of gameland, for deer and other game are found in large numbers within a few miles." This hotel, like the Alpine, was dismantled piece by piece, during the early 1960s.

The Deer Park Hotel

The Deer Park Hotel was considered North Woodstock's leading inn. Built in 1886–1887, it boasted "a good golf course, an orchestra, and all the attractions to be usually found in a first-class resort." It remained open until 1952.

This view, looking north up Main Street, shows the business district of North Woodstock. The traditional bandstand is at the lower left, and Franconia Notch is in the distance.

The Alpine

The Alpine was built in 1890–1891 on an elevation overlooking the Pemigewasset Valley. It offered guests a magnificent view of mountains and valleys and plenty of pure and invigorating mountain air. The publication *Among the Clouds* described the hotel as follows: "The house is well planned. Every guest room is a front room, with two large windows, running water, telephone, twin beds, hardwood floors, beautiful rugs, and furnishings. The office or lobby is large with a massive stone fireplace, around which are drawn a number of comfortable chairs. Adjoining it are the ladies writing room, small parlors, dance hall, men's smoking room, and a barber shop. All the new public rooms are handsomely furnished and decorated, with large art squares covering the floors. The dining room is one of the many attractions, with its large plate glass windows and seating capacity for 300 guests." The hotel did not succumb to fire as did so many of the early hotels but rather was demolished in 1966.

The Mountain Park House

The Mountain Park House was built *c.* the 1880s. Information about the hotel appeared in the 1902 *Tourists' Guide-Book for the State of New Hampshire:* "There is a broad piazza on three sides of the house, both on the ground and second floors, from which can be seen Tucker and Sawyer's Mountains, Waternomee, Pemigewasset, Kinsman, Profile; also view of Franconia Notch, Mount Russell, Loon Pond Mountain, Mount Hicks, Collidge mountains, Mounts Haystack, Flume, Liberty, Lincoln, and Lafayette. There is an excellent trout brook on the farm, within a stone's throw of the hotel. Directly opposite on the top of Mount Russell, is a

Like many hotels in the White Mountains, the Alpine Hotel was a family operation. With room for more than 200 guests, the Alpine was open from June to October. This view dates from c. 1916.

The Mountain Park House was open from June to November, with accommodations for 40 guests.

Open year-round, the Russell House was a modest hotel that accommodated up to 65 guests.

beautiful expanse of water, known as Lake Russell, and to the westward, situated on the top of Mount Scilly, is Elbow Lake. Both of these lakes are easy of access, and abound in different kinds of fish, making it especially attractive to the tourist. Game is abundant in the woods."

The Russell House

The Russell House was built *c.* 1875 and remained in operation until *c.* 1942. This house is advertised in the *Tourists' Guide-Book for the State of New Hampshire* as: "a year round resort house situated at the gateway to the Franconia and White Mountain Ranges in the midst of the most picturesque mountain, valley, river, and lake scenery, is pronounced by experienced travelers to stand unrivaled in natural and enjoyable attractions. Surrounded by hills secluded roads, lovely walks, drives over roads winding along banks of swift brooks through forests and over hills, each with its distinctive features of interest and history. This house, built with an especial regard to wants of summer boarders, has liberal accommodations for fifty guests."

Today, lining the main street are small hotels, motels, elegant resorts, restaurants, antiques stores, and gift shops. It is here at North Woodstock that the East Branch of the Pemigewasset, coming down from the Pemigewasset wilderness, unites with the Pemigewasset River and Lost River, forming the spot known as the Three Rivers, a favorite subject for landscape painters.

While groups of tourists were coming to the North Country for relaxation and entertainment, other groups were entering the mountains for an entirely different reason: lumbering the woods and the wilderness. The Gordon Pond Railroad and the Woodstock–Thornton Gore Railroad were in full use from 1906 to 1916. The Woodstock Lumber Company

The industrial lumber town of Woodstock nestles in the Pemigewasset Valley. The view, looking northeast, was taken from Bald Ledge.

The village of North Woodstock is especially noted for the beauty of its surroundings—the Pemigewasset Valley, the forests, and the mountains.

brought many jobs and more people to town. In 1912, large-scale lumbering in the area ended with the purchase of the large Lost River Reservation in the Kinsman Notch and, by 1917, through the purchase of the land by the federal government to create the White Mountain National Forest. From 1885 to 1910, conservationists had crusaded for a preserve in the White Mountains. The White Mountain National Forest Reserve was established in 1911 after public outcry forced passage of the Weeks Act, allowing the federal government to purchase private land east of the Mississippi River. The White Mountains National Forest was established in 1918 by a presidential proclamation.

The New Hampshire Land Company

In 1893, the J.E. Henry logging operation in the Lincoln wilderness opened the Pemigewasset countryside to outside investors. With the advent of the Pemigewasset Valley Railroad (later the Boston & Maine), the logging industry experienced a boom. In the valley, George B. James and his New Hampshire Land Company stripped the slopes of some of the best timber in the Northeast. Although Henry was neither a logger nor a railroad man, he saw the ripe virgin land as a good investment for a logging industry. His New Hampshire Land Company played an important role in the White Mountain logging industry.

The New Hampshire Land Company (1880–1905) was incorporated in 1880 with its field office in Plymouth and its home office in Boston, Massachusetts. The elaborate prospectus, printed in 1880 by the G.H. Ellis of Boston, stated that some of the company's major purposes were to develop a lumber business in Grafton, Carroll, and Coos Counties; to purchase desirable blocks of timberland for sale at low prices; to sell the standing timber or stumpage, and to construct, operate, or lease the narrow-gauge railroads for lumbering and mountain travel. At the very outset of this operation, the company claimed more than 240,000 acres of virgin forest in the towns of Livermore, Franconia, Lincoln, Bethlehem, Woodstock, Sandwich, Waterville, Ellsworth, Thornton, and other locations, grants, and gores. More than half of these acquisitions came from state agents as a result of the 1867 Legislative Resolve. At this time it is probable that only the U.S. government (working to establish titles to the White Mountain National Forest) appears more often in White Mountain land transactions than does the New Hampshire Land Company.

The following excerpt is from C. Francis Belcher's *Logging Railroads of the White Mountains:*

> In their lifetime, James and Company knew and dealt with the biggest, the roughest, and the most urbane: George Van Dyke, James E. Henry, Daniel Saunders & Sons, George Johnson, Oakleigh Thorne, A. Crosby Kennett, and even the non-rail loggers, the Daniels of the Winnepesogee and International Paper Companies. For better or worse, James was the essential catalyst then funneled the hundreds of land units to the loggers in big enough bites for them to swallow and digest efficiently. Passaconaway, Woodstock, Thornton Gore, Agassiz Basin, and the Beebe River country lost their many loving natives and their forest cover, thanks to the New Hampshire Land Company, and its president.
>
> His land dealings in the Pemigewasset country earned him notorious titles from the angry writings of Rev. John E. Johnson, a summer resident of the Pemigewasset Valley, and later a substantial benefactor of the Dartmouth Outing Club. In an article written for the December 1900 issue of *National Single Taxer,* and later widely reprinted elsewhere as a book and article, Rev. Johnson called the New Hampshire Land Company and its president "The Boar Constrictor of the White Mountains," or the "Worst Trust in the World."
>
> It was widely known that James and his New Hampshire Land Company were never considered loggers for they had never operated a sawmill or ran a logging locomotive. It is interesting to note that from the files of the Suffolk County Probate Court in

With snow covering the ground, the mill crew of the Johnson Lumber Company poses outside. Logging camps dotted the Kinsman and wilderness areas.

A trainload of logs arrives from Lost River. Even during the winter months, logging operations continued throughout the wilderness.

Massachusetts for insolvency on Oct. 14, 1925, the following: "The debts and liabilities of their client, George B. James, who had died February 23, 1924, far exceeded the assets in their hands."

The Gordon Pond Railroad (1907-1916)

In 1896, the new Whitehouse, Hall, and Burns Branch Railroad was extended approximately six miles north from North Woodstock. The work was accomplished under the Boston & Maine Railroad's authority to construct a continuing extension of its Pemigewasset Valley Branch to the Frank Hall sawmill near the Flume House.

C. Francis Belcher, in his book *Logging Railroads in the White Mountains,* makes the following observations:

> Freight receipts for it were not exceptional until George L. Johnson of Monroe established a sawmill in a section of Lincoln west of this branch in 1904. Quite soon Johnson had this section of Lincoln west of Rte. 3 along the Harvard Brook named for him and was appointed postmaster of Johnson.
>
> On May 1, 1908, Johnson officially leased two and one-half miles of the Whitehouse Branch from the Boston & Maine Railroad to start the wheels rolling on his infant Gordon Pond Railroad, incorporated by the New Hampshire Legislature in 1907. Actually, Johnson was never a large landowner, owning about 6,000 acres along the Harvard and Gordon Pond brook near his village and mill. During this period from 1904 to 1908, he had done his first cutting to pay off loans to the always-present J.E. Henry. In this period, for one year only, the Boston & Maine had agreed to allow Johnson to run his trains to Henry's mill subject to Boston & Maine order.

In 1906, the Publishers Paper Company negotiated with the Johnson Company in selling the Lost River mill. George L. Johnson did very well; his shay engines became quite busy. Because Lost River was a unique attraction, his operations were carefully viewed by all, especially the conservationists.

Karl P. Harrington, in his *Walks and Climbs in the White Mountains,* writes: "From this point on, the hauling of logs ruined the consistency of the road, and we crawled up the hill in sawdust, sank halfway to the hubs in mud holes, crept over shaky bridges, vainly endeavored to dodge shapeless rocks, and at length gave up the attempt to ride . . . On arrival at the point in the road where we must leave it for the gorge (Lost River), we found ourselves in the midst of a wilderness of devastation, dead tree tops, felled logs, and a network of abandoned roads.

The following excerpt from *Appalachia, Volume XI,* pages 53–54 (1907) records an early attempt to save Lost River.

> There was brought to our attention in the autumn by the Councilor of Improvements the grave and impending danger of the destruction of the forest in the Lost River region in North Woodstock, and the matter was taken at once into serious consideration. After considerable correspondence, it was ascertained that the Publishers' Paper Co. of Portsmouth . . . is the owner of the land, and that the cutting is being done by the Johnson paper Co. of Johnson . . . Upon inspection of the premises, it appears that the cutting of the forest had come already to the very borders of the Lost River, and that a wood road was in process of construction to enable this also to be reached. Owing to the obligations between the two companies, it was a difficult matter to come to any satisfactory arrangement, as each company naturally feared that any deviation from the terms of its contract, however slight, might give rise to litigation." The article continues: "no cutting now will take place during this winter, at least, upon an area of approximately twenty-three (23) acres, extending between the state road and a

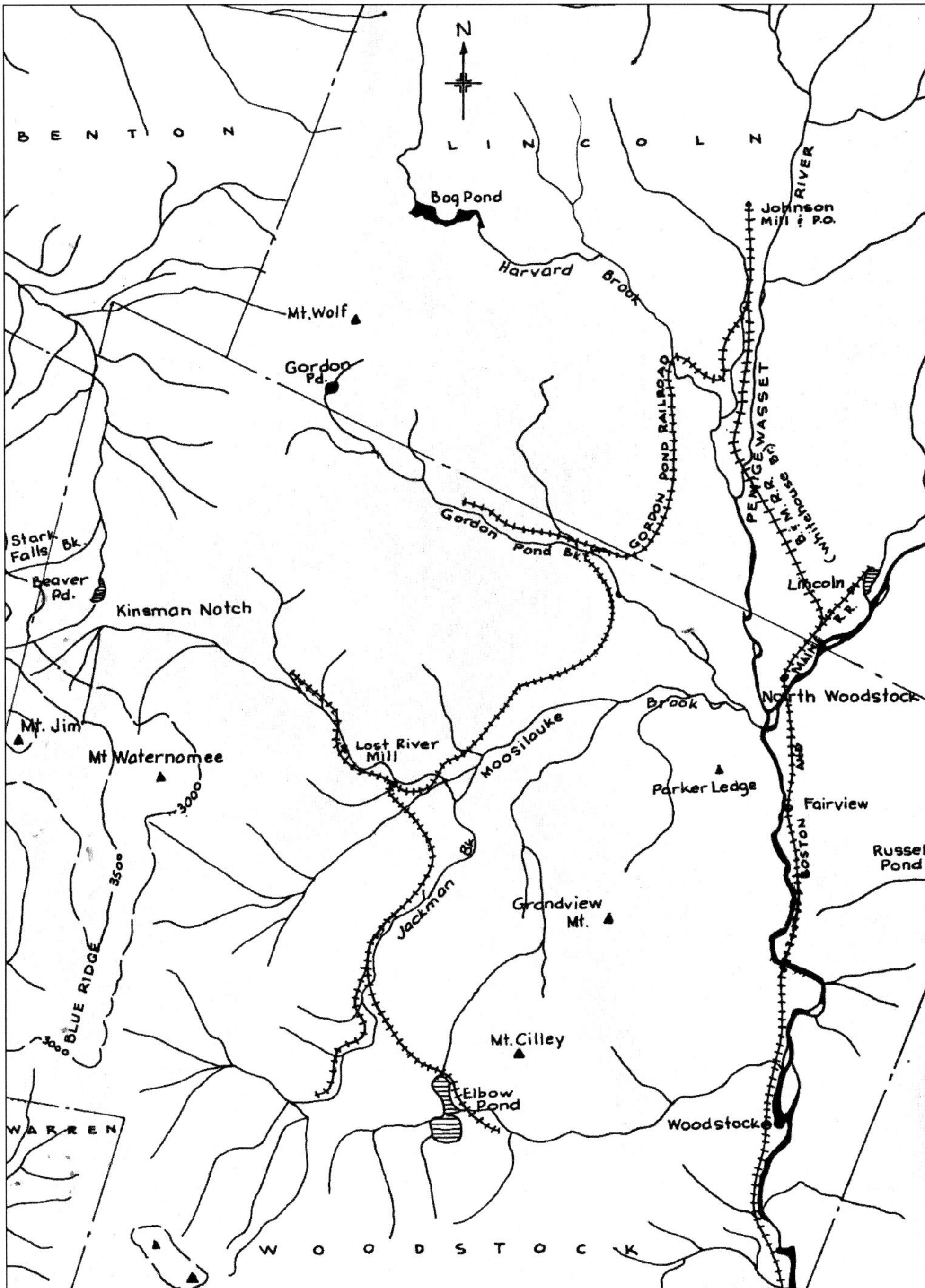

This map shows the extent of logging operations in the Lost River area in 1910.

Shown is the Woodstock Lumber Company, one of many mills that once operated in the Pemigewasset Valley.

> straight line about 500 feet northeasterly there from, and in length about 1,800 feet. It is possible some arrangement may be made by which the ownership of this most interesting region may be acquired by the Club.

The National Forest

As early as February 1893, Julius H. Ward published an article entitled "White Mountain Forest in Peril" in the *Atlantic Monthly*, sounding a note of warning, telling of the wasteful and destructive lumbering—"unwise and barbarous," he characterized it—giving a number of typical instances of the results of such cutting, and asserting that a few lumbermen have it in their power "to spoil the whole White Mountains region for a period of fifty years, to dry up the East Branch of the Pemigewasset, to reduce the Merrimack to the size of a brook in summer, and to bring about a desolation like that which surrounds Jerusalem in the Holy Land." The protection and preservation of these forests should be regarded as a national problem, he declared, the White Mountains with their forests being "worth infinitely more for the purpose of a great national park than for the temporary supply of lumber which they furnish to the market."

F. W. Rollins, President. **Joseph T. Walker,** Secretary. **George T. Cruft,** Treasurer. **Philip W. Ayres,** Forester.

The Society FOR THE PROTECTION OF New Hampshire Forests

SAVE THE FORESTS

The Society for the Protection of New Hampshire Forests prepared a bill which was passed by the New Hampshire Legislature last winter inviting the Bureau of Forestry at Washington to make a thorough examination of the White Mountain region. This examination is now well under way. The Society desires to use the knowledge thus gained in making an appeal to Congress next winter for a National Forest Reservation in the White Mountains and asks your aid in so doing. The plan has the emphatic endorsement of President Roosevelt, Secretary John Hay, and members of Congress from New Hampshire and other states.

Memberships in the Society are as follows:

Patron Member, - - $100.00
Life Member, - - - - 25.00
Sustaining Member, annually, 10.00
Contributing Member, - - 5.00
Annual Member, - - - 1.00

Checks may be made payable to George T. Cruft, Treasurer, and sent to Bethlehem, N. H., or to 5 Tremont Street, Boston, Mass.

The Society for the Protection of New Hampshire Forests put out this notice in an effort to increase its membership.

Cutting Regulation

He went on to suggest that if the one or two large owners should adopt the regulation, already followed by one company, of cutting no trees below 12 inches at the butt, they would practically settle the problem. His idea was that the state, through a forest commission, should purchase from the owners of woodland in certain regions an agreement that they would not cut trees below a certain size.

Other writers took up the crusade to preserve the White Mountains forests, and, aided by the establishment of a scientific forest program by the national government and by the popular interest taken in the subject of conservation, a campaign in favor of a forest reservation in the region was launched and, before long, gained support nationwide.

White Mountains Reserve

On January 10, 1903, the New Hampshire legislature passed a bill, favoring the proposal to establish a White Mountains reserve and giving the state's consent to the acquisition by purchase, gift, or condemnation of lands that the federal government decided might be needed for the purpose.

At the same session, the legislature authorized and directed the State Forestry Commission to have the Department of Agriculture's Bureau of Forestry examine the forest lands of the White Mountains. To protect this and other vast tracts of land in the White Mountains from private logging operations, landslides and fire, the Society for Protection of New Hampshire Forests was established.

The "Progress Report of 1912" that appears in Helenette Silver's *New Hampshire Game and Furbearers*, published by the New Hampshire Fish and Game Department (1957), includes the following: "The work of the United States government for suppression of fires in the White Mountain region has been accomplished under the direction of Mr. Hirst, the State Forester. The government duplicates the state's appropriation for this purpose, and expanded $7,200 in 1911, and $8,000, in 1912, for preventing fires in the mountain region. The chief activities of the Timberland Owners' Association in Northern New Hampshire have been to co-operate with the State Forester and the government in the suppression of forest fires."

In the same report, the section titled "Purchase and Improvement at Lost River" states in part, "At a cost of $6,597 the To protect this and other vast tracts of land in the White Mountains from private logging operations, landslides and fire, the Society for Protection of New Hampshire Forests was established. purchased the timber on 148 acres surrounding Lost River. Besides considerable cut-over land, the tract contains nearly one million feet of merchantable spruce timber of large size. This is located upon the steep bluff overhanging the river. The Publishers Paper Company contributed the tract of land, but the Society paid for the timber. The price is a high one, but the sub-contractors under the Publishers Paper Company were proceeding to cut the timber off, and it was necessary to rescue it immediately. A claim to an undivided one-third interest in the lot upon which the caverns are located was generously contributed by the International Paper Company. Upon the purchase, the Society expended $1,200 towards the improvements at Lost River - cleared debris left by the lumbering operations, built bridges, and repaired the road connecting Woodstock to Lost River with the assistance of the Town of Woodstock so that visitors may safely reach the Lost River."

The report concluded with a note of appreciation to groups that assisted: the Woman's Club of New Hampshire for contributing $625, the Concord club, and the Plymouth, Hinsdale, and Lisbon clubs for their work.

White Mountain Protection

In February 1911, the 61st Congress passed a bill for the protection of the White Mountain forests. The bill became law when Pres. William Howard Taft signed it on March 1, 1911.

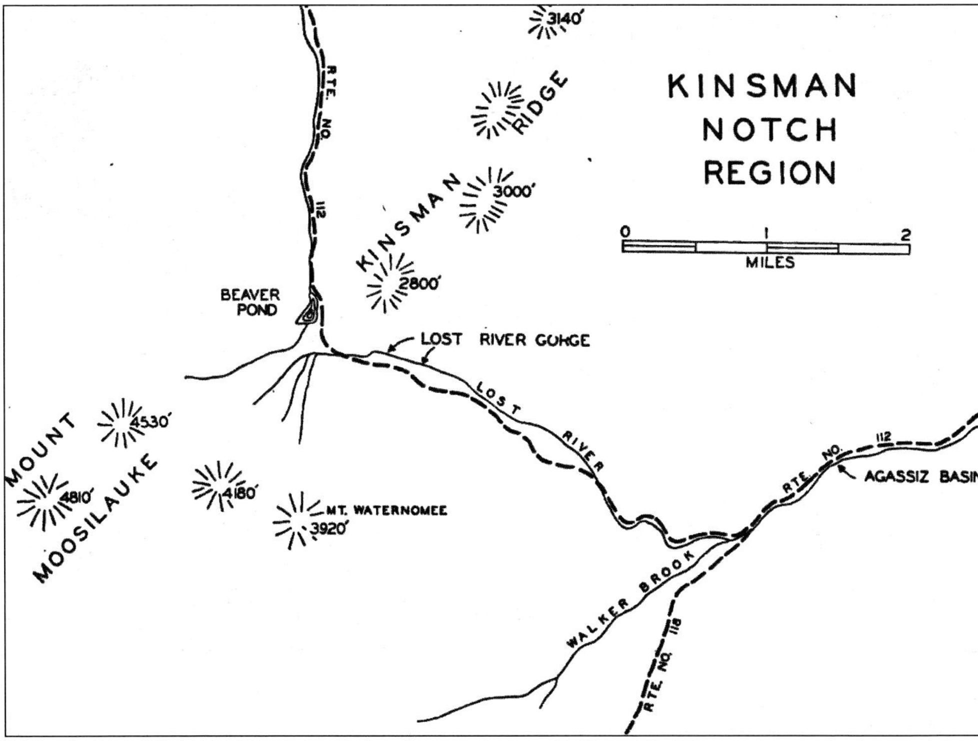

This map shows the Kinsman Notch region.

The view west into Kinsman Notch shows the forested beauty of the Lost River area.

Kinsman Notch

The Kinsman Notch lies within the Mount Moosilauke and the Kinsman Ranges, forming a natural pass between the Pemigewasset and Connecticut River Valleys. One half of it descends from the artificial Beaver Pond near the top of the notch almost due northward and drains into the headwaters of the wild Ammonoosuc River. At an elevation of 1,880 feet, is a low, broad divide in the floor of the notch known as the "height of land." From this divide, the Lost River flows southeastward through Agassiz Basin to join the Pemigewasset River at North Woodstock. The lesser peaks of the Moosilauke and Kinsman Ranges rise from 1,000 to 3,000 feet above the notch floor, and three miles to the southwest lies the summit of Moosilauke, at 4,810 feet, the highest of the southern White Mountains.

The Kinsman Notch takes its name from an early pioneer, Asa Kinsman, who hewed his way through the Notch with an ax rather than turn back when he found himself on the wrong road. He is said to have come from the south, with his wife and household goods piled on a two-wheeled cart pulled by a yoke of oxen, bound for Landaff to take up a land grant. When he and his wife arrived in Woodstock (Peeling), they found they were on the wrong track and that Landaff was beyond the lofty mountain, nine miles farther northwest. Undaunted, the couple proceeded to cut their way through the forest, with the help of two strangers, in order to reach the Landaff, where they eventually made their home.

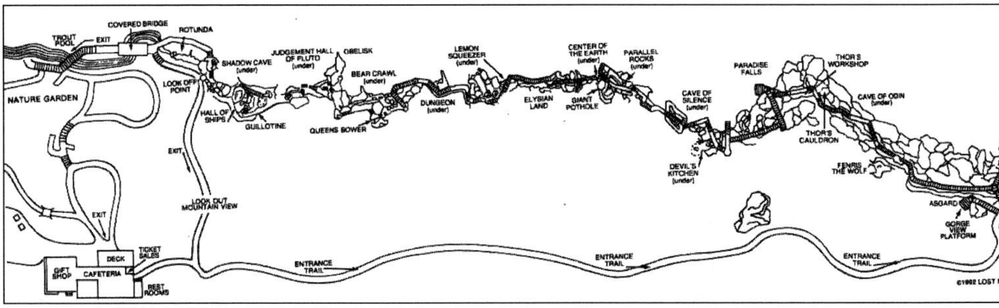

The Lost River Reservation contains some 148 acres and includes well-designed walkways through narrow passages between gigantic rocks.

Lost River

Lost River is so named because the stream that drains the southern part of Kinsman Notch disappears and goes below the surface for a quarter of a mile in a narrow, steep-walled glacial gorge. The secluded ravine, located approximately six miles northwest of North Woodstock, is partially filled by immense blocks of granite, and the natural brook cascades and flows through the spaces between the granite blocks.

Legend has it that some 50 years after Asa Kinsman, cut his way through the notch, two boys named Royal and Lyman Jackman went fishing in this area. Suddenly, Lyman disappeared "as though the earth had opened and swallowed him." He had dropped down approximately 12 feet through a hole into a waist-high pool. Badly frightened but unhurt, Lyman was fished out by Royal. Many years afterward, Royal came back to North Woodstock to visit and, accompanied by a group of boys, found his way through the woods to the present Cave of Shadows, where he and his brother had found the Lost River.

Only since 1895 has Lost River been generally known to the public. Its exploration is no easy task, but a careful examination of this hidden product of nature's mysterious and prehistoric convulsion reveals wonders: caverns, waterfalls, huge blocks of granite, the numerous and enormous potholes, and deep recesses through which the stream flows in darkness. The gorge is rated, along with the Profile and the Flume, as the one of the three most interesting natural features of the Franconia Mountains. From a geological and historical point of view, the Lost River gorge holds more fascination than anything of a like nature in New Hampshire or possibly in all of New England. The following is a narrative journey made by Justis Conrad in 1912:

> Among the thousand times, and possibly more, that I have explored Lost River, I have yet to learn of one that did not feel highly repaid for the journey.
>
> The gorge is entered at the northern end where the stream plunges beneath huge boulders and is lost from view and is not seen again except in caverns until it appears on the exterior at "Elysian Land." Passing over a series of bridges and ladders the visitor descends to "The Hall of Ships," thirty feet below point of entrance. This a deep, narrow gorge resembling somewhat "The Flume" of Franconia Notch, and gets its name from a large boulder that resembles the stern of a ship leaving port. The next is a "presto chango" act through a small tunnel into "Shadow Cave." This is a large room in which fifty people can gather, and by use of a torch view the little river as it glides along beneath large boulders on the northern side. At certain times of the day the light that comes in through the crevices enables one to see his shadow in the water, hence the name. From this point we ascend a ladder and come to the exterior where with

Lost River is a gorge not far south of the divide in Kinsman Notch.

Below the entrance of Lost River is the Hall of Ships.

a shudder we view "The Guillotine" and pass swiftly on down, down over another series of ladders into "The Judgment Hall of Pluto," which is fifty feet lower than the point of entrance to the gorge. This is a room in which the river again appears in the shape of a large pool. The architecture of this room is magnificent, boulders of every conceivable size and shape hanging from overhead. What is it we hear? We listen, look, a torch is lighted, we rush forward. There at the northern end of the hall, back behind a gigantic boulder, the "Falls of Proserpine" are tumbling for twenty feet, while we are showered with a cooling mist. We retreat up, up the ladder and on through the "Cave of the Shades" and thence into "The Dungeon" and rest in "The Hall of Lethe" (forgetfulness). Here the shadows thrown upon the water of the dungeon by the sunlight streaming down through the deep crevices produce a most beautiful picture.

Again we retreat up a long ladder and emerge into "Elysian Land" on the exterior, where the river glides gracefully along among the moss covered rocks soon to be lost, however, in the "The Center of the Earth Cave." Again we pass over a series of well-kept walks and bridges through "Elysian Land" and hide ourselves in the "King's Chamber," from whence we can view by the use of a torch the deep pool in the "Center of the Earth Cave." This is a large cave in which a small boat could float.

We pass next to the "Giant's Pot Hole" which from a geological point of view is one of the chief wonders of the gorge. Here we rest and wonder, and then pass on through "The Narrows" and into the "Cave of Silence." While not so picturesque as the others, this cave is in some respects the most impressive of any of the series, on account of the deep stillness. Not a sound of the river can be heard except the distant murmur of the falls as the water escapes from its long imprisonment farther down the gorge. It is at this point that the river is so much lost that no one as yet has been able to absolutely determine its exact course.

We now enter the "Cave of Lost Souls" and, while the name might make us shudder, we continue on and find that this is a continuous series of rooms accessible to any that do not mind a hard stunt. All things considered, this is the most wonderful cave in the gorge. Retreating from this cave, we climb to the "Upper Bridge" that spans the gorge twenty feet above the bottom. From this point we look into "The Gulf" forty feet below into which the waters of "Paradise Falls" tumbles perpendicularly for twenty feet. [Paradise Falls is formed by Lost River flowing over two parallel pegmatite dikes. These are more resistant to abrasion than the granite, so they hold up the brook in much the same way as an artificial dam. The basin, at the foot of the falls, is an irregularly shaped pothole scoured out of the granite and partly filled with fallen blocks of rock.]

Eventually, we pass to the "Lower Bridge" that spans the gulf, from whence we view the "Long Lost River" as it emerges from the "Cave of Silence" and the other caves beyond. This view, looking up the gorge, is pronounced by many to be the most picturesque of any. We now ascend from the gorge through a winding path to "Point Lookoff." It is here that a magnificent view of Kinsman Notch and the distant Waterville Range can be had. No notch in the White Mountains affords such a grand distant view as does Kinsman Notch at Point Lookoff.

The waters of Paradise Falls cascade into the Gulf.

Agassiz Basin was named in honor of geologist Louis Agassiz, who first recognized that ice sheets formerly covered large parts of the Northern Hemisphere.

Agassiz Basin

Agassiz Basin is located in the bed of Lost River, four miles southeast of the Lost River Gorge. The basin is an irregular stream channel that was cut into massive ledges of Kinsman granite at approximately the same time as Lost River Gorge. The narrowest part of the gorge occurs where a pegmatite dike extends across it. The dike is more resistant to stream abrasion than the granite and has not been widened. Where it crosses the river, a narrow cascade forms. Several small potholes occur above water level on the west side of the gorge. These were probably cut at an early stage of the basin erosion, and as the stream channel was lowered they were abandoned on the flank of the gorge.

Three quarters of a mile northwest of the Lost River Gorge is the Beaver Pond area of Kinsman Notch. Around the pond are several features which shed some light on the geologic history of the notch. One such feature, a ledge of Littleton schist beside the highway approximately 100 yards north of the end of Beaver Pond, shows prominent parallel grooves and scratches. The grooves were ground out as the glacier dragged boulders over the ledge, which consists of contorted schists, recrystallized sand, and mud of the Littleton formation. The ledge is one of the most accessible outcrops of this type of rock near the Lost River. The ledges at the north end of Beaver Pond, at the dam, consist of typical Kinsman granite, which contains narrow pegmatite dikes and large blocks of Littleton schist. Some of the blocks have narrow borders of different color and texture, due to their partial assimilation by the granite. An abandoned gravel bank on the east side of the highway at the north end of Beaver Pond contains stratified, waterworn gravel. This material was deposited by water high in the Kinsman Notch when the ice was melting out of the notch, but while the glacial meltwater was pouring southward through the notch and eroding the Lost River Gorge.

The Mount Moosilauke House was located on a spur of Mount Moosilauke at an elavation of 1,700 feet above sea level. The three-and-a-half-story structure could accommodate 100 guests.

Mount Moosilauke

Southwest of the Beaver Pond and Mount Kinsman stands Mount Moosilauke. Almost isolated from the Kinsman Mountain Range, it affords a superb view and has the advantage of being easily accessible. *The Book of the White Mountains*, by John Anderson and Sterns Morse (1930), describes the panoramic view from the summit of Moosilauke: "From the summit of Moosilauke Mount Washington may be found to the northeast by sighting along a line drawn to the right of Mount Liberty, the more northerly of two mountains of similar shape across Franconia Notch, and to the left of Mount Bond, some six miles beyond Liberty. Once this commanding landmark is identified the observer can readily find the others. Mount Jefferson is to the left of Washington and Adams back of Jefferson; to the north stretch the long wooded slopes of Mount Kinsman."

The Moosilauke House, positioned high upon the spur of Mount Moosilauke, commanded a full view of the Pemigewasset Valley and the western horizon of the White Mountains. During its existence, from 1886 to 1953, the hotel was also known as the Moosilauke Inn and the Breezy Point House. It advertised that "Mountain springs supply an abundance of the purest water; the sanitary arrangements are excellent, and miles of walks are included in the estate." The Moosilauke House was considered one of the most stylish hotels in the White Mountains, even though it was not of the large proportions of a grand hotel.

Visitors view the Giant's Pothole, one of the wonders of the Lost River gorge.

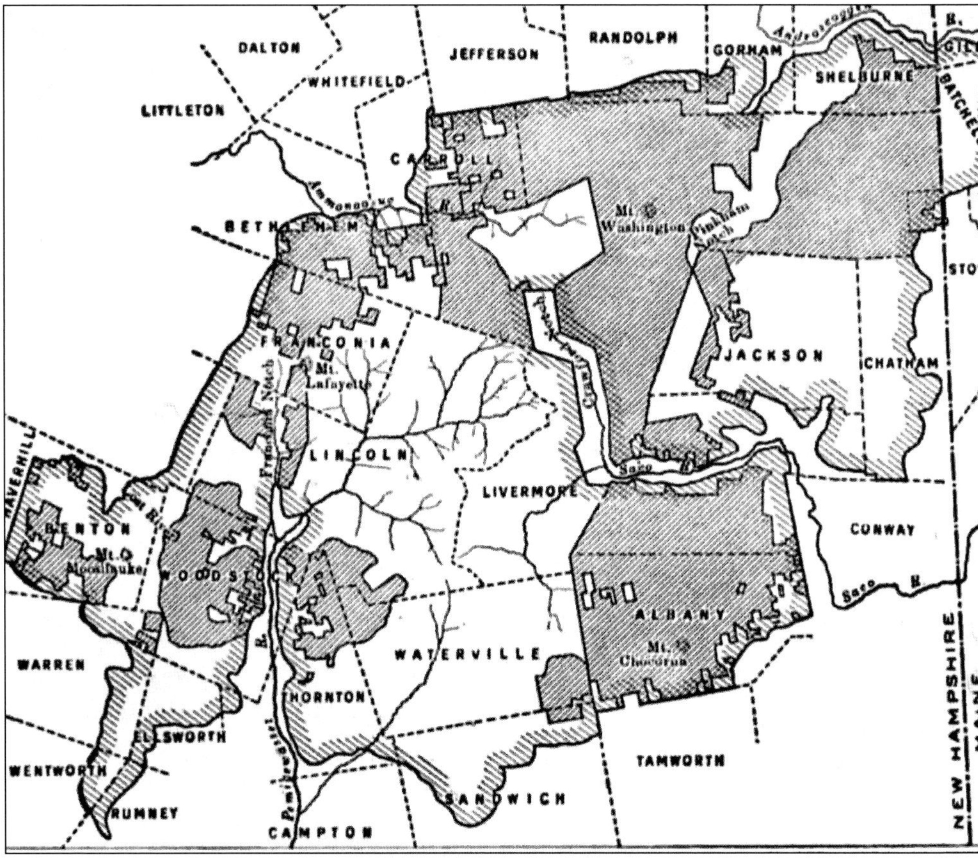

From 1885 to 1910, conservationists crusaded for a preserve in the White Mountains. The White Mountain National Forest Reserve was established in 1911, after public outcry forced passage of the Weeks Act, allowing the federal government to purchase private land east of the Mississippi River. The White Mountains National Forest was established in 1918 by a presidential proclamation. The shaded areas of this early 1900s map show the 698,000-acre reserve originally planned. The total amount of land acquired as of September 1998 was approximately 728,150 acres.

Seven
Lincoln

North of Woodstock is the town of Lincoln. The middle branch of the Pemigewasset River flows southward through the central part of town, and the East Branch of the river flows through the eastern part of town, which is known as the Pemigewasset wilderness. The town was granted on January 31, 1764, to James Avery and others in 71 equal shares with a total area of 32,456 acres. The landscape was extremely rough and mountainous—unsuitable for farming but well endowed with fish, timber, animals, fowl, and adventure. Settlement did not get under way here until after the close of the Revolution. As late as 1791, Lincoln had only 22 settlers and very few farms existed on the 1,000 acres of improved land. During Colonial days, royal grants specified that Lincoln contained an abundance of white pine and other pine trees "fit for masting our Royal Navy" that were to be carefully preserved for that use. Under British law the cutting of any of these trees, which were marked with the broad royal arrow, was a felony punishable by a heavy fine and by forfeiture of all rights of the grantee and his heirs and assigns. So vast were the forests in Pemigewasset Valley and lower slopes of the mountains that the supply of timber seemed inexhaustible. No thought of a possible future scarcity ever occurred to the early settlers or lumbermen; thus, more care was not taken by them in the cutting of the timber.

As the country built up, the loggers began to branch out, looking for the best pine. For a long time, cutting was limited to areas accessible by waterways where lumber could be transported downriver to the sawmills. At that time transportation was so difficult that only the choicest timber had any commercial value. For miles the larger rivers, such as the Pemigewasset, were a solid stream of logs, kept in place by long boom chains attached to rock-filled river cribs. At the local mills along the Pemigewasset, the logs were hoisted from the water onto an escalator conveyor that threw them like matchsticks to the top of a mountainous stockpile.

In 1813, the state of New Hampshire built a road through Franconia Notch, making the White Mountains easily accessible to the northern communities in the Connecticut River Valley. The principal occupation of the townspeople became the care of tourists, and inns and hotels opened along the roadways. The first hotel was built by Stephen Russell in 1808, a short distance below the Flume, a primary goal of early travelers and sightseers. The first Flume House was built in 1848 on the main road about a mile from the gorge. After it burned in 1871, the hotel was immediately rebuilt by Taft and Greenleaf at a cost of $32,000 and was reopened for in 1872. The hotel did so well that, in 1883, an addition was built to double its capacity. The Flume House burned in 1918 and was not rebuilt.

The first significant industry was established in 1859 by Henry Baker, who moved to Lincoln with his family from Vermont. Baker bought land from Stephen Russell and transformed Russell's mill into a bedstead factory. During the 1860s, Baker turned his business to the production of chair backs. Another of the early factories was a sawmill called

This view of the Franconia Range was taken looking north from the summit of Loon Mountain in Lincoln. From this vantage point, the logging area is clearly visible.

Whitehouse, located above the bridge by that name. A small settlement grew around it with about 20 families and a school.

In 1880, Lincoln had a sparse population of 66 settlers. In 1885, the town had two school districts and two common schools. Its two schoolhouses accommodated two teachers instructing 17 students. At that time, there was no village or post office.

J.E. Henry & Sons

In 1892, everything changed and another era began. James E. Henry, his sons, and others arrived and established a logging industry in Lincoln. At that time, the town was known as Pollard's for its mountain lodge where up to 20 guests were put up for $1 a day, the adventurous ones receiving a guided tour of the great wilderness of the East Branch from Dura Pollard. The J.E. Henry & Sons logging settlement received early mention in the following article written for the *Granite Monthly* by George Moses: "Pullman, New Hampshire—you may not find it on your map; you may not mail a letter to that address and have it delivered; no enterprising scalper may sell you a reduced railroad ticket to that destination; yet it exists and there is some basis of the fact for my fancy in thus titling the lumber town of Lincoln on the East Branch of the Pemigewasset . . . But this is digression. On the first of September 1892, where now stands the lumber town of Lincoln was a dense, virgin forest. A year later the village of Lincoln with a school, store, dwellings, shops, and mills was visible evidence to all. It had sprung up almost over night through the boundless energy and unflagging courage of its owners, who in fact of a steadily falling market, deepened their investment and increased their risk."

In an article written for the *Northeastern Logger*, a J.E. Henry employee named Jim Doherty recollects the following: "That day in August 1892, we drove over from the other side, down through the notch. There was quite a party of us, Mr. Henry, his sons, George, John, Charlie, and others, as well as the womenfolk and the children. Well, the day after we got here we all went to work clearing land, building houses, and putting in a railroad . . . During the fall we had 100 to 150 men working and by winter we had finished six houses, a store, a barn, a blacksmith shop, and harness shop. Besides that, we had cleared a lot of land, and made a start on the railroad, so that by March, two miles of railroad were finished and the logs started rolling into Lincoln. Then a portable sawmill was set up and the lumber sawed for more houses which were built along Main Street for the big sawmill which in a few more months was completed and was turning out a hundred thousand feet a day of sawed lumber. It was a hard winter, four or five feet of snow and lots of cold weather. The houses were little more than shacks, but we were all packed in so tight that everyone managed to keep warm."

Reaction

Residents of the neighboring town of North Woodstock were not happy with the new inhabitants of Pollard's wilderness, as noted in three issues of the *White Mountain Echo*. August 4, 1894: "Can it be that this fair region is to become as sad a scene of desolation as that which Zealand Valley now presents to the eye?" August 11, 1894: "The wealthy lumber king has been among us a year and has his work of devastation well under way. He is not a lumberman, but a wood-butcher, a mutilator of nature, a destroyer of the property of a thousand for the benefit of himself. The bare unsightly sides of Black Mountain, the dwindling streams and barren slopes of Collidge, all testify against him." September 1, 1894: "Early on Saturday morning the party [American Forestry Association] proceeded by the Pemigewasset Valley Railroad to North Woodstock, whence they continued by a special train to the lumber camps of the Messrs. J.E. Henry & Sons at Lincoln, where they were presented with an object lesson of not the most pleasing character."

In the course of time, the J.E. Henry organization became increasingly powerful in the operation and control of this logging town. The new settlement was his. The company rented the homes to its employees, established a company store, provided the town with ice and electricity, and eventually built a hospital. James E. Henry, himself, was the local judge and, in 1902, his son John Henry was appointed the first postmaster of Lincoln. In 1903, the Henrys built their own hotel, the Lincoln House.

George Moses wrote the following observations of life in Henry's town for the *Granite Monthly* (1895):

> It is not a perfect town by any means, yet it is superior in all it managerial features. This is a necessary fact because the town is designed to supply the needs which were purely managerial . . . The government and discipline are, as one might suppose, intensely paternal and the administration is most rigid. The old town of Lincoln lies off to the west from '*The Grand Duchy*', and the population is aligned along the highway leading northward to the Franconia Notch. The selectman and other town officials are therefore chosen from among the older inhabitants to enforce whatever regulations they deem necessary to the peace and dignity of their grand ducal estate. Prohibition is the rule in our Pullman [Lincoln], and it does prohibit. The labor accomplished daily by the Henrys, father and sons, comes nothing short of Herculean. 'The Old Man' Henry, as he is known from the Pemigewasset to the St. Lawrence, has lived a life of almost unremitting toil, and the dignity of labor is a family tenet with him.
>
> When one recalls that the number of hands employed in this New Hampshire Pullman are many times as numerous as the entire body of original inhabitants and that they are dependent for everything upon the inclinations of the owners of the village, the possibilities by way of politics are highly suggestive. And when one thinks of the agitation for the preservation of the forest of the White Mountains Region among whose foothills this forest lies, there is suggested the boundless opportunity which the Messrs. Henry have of demonstrating how to use and at the same time to preserve the valuable growth.

On the back of the passes issued to the Henry company workers is printed the follow description of Lincoln: "Lincoln . . . is one mile from the town of North Woodstock on the Concord & Montreal Railroad. It is one of the largest firms in the state. A good man can find work all year. A poor man better not go there, as such men are not wanted."

The East Branch & Lincoln Railroad (1893–1948)

The East Branch & Lincoln Railroad began as a standard-gauge line. The first two engines were Baldwin-built, 35-tonners imported from the Zealand line over the Concord & Montreal main line via Woodstock and Plymouth. The railroad became a systematic operation, distinguished by the high-grade construction of its main line of tracks and the quality of its cars. J.E. Henry & Sons planned their right-of-way well, particularly on the main stem between Lincoln and North Fork Junction, still evident along the four-mile section of the Kancamagus Highway from Lincoln to the Wilderness Trail.

New construction of the railroad, camps, roads, and the many other physical features of the line were undertaken during the summer seasons when little major cutting was under way. The Henry lumber camps were much the same as other camps: they were made primarily of boards rather than logs, and they transported their camp building from place to place by means of the railroad.

Threat of Fire

One of the major concerns J.E. Henry had was the threat of fire. On May 13, 1907, his worst fears were realized. As C. Francis Belcher reports in *Logging Railroads of the White Mountains,* "At high noon one of [the] switching engines belched some stray sparks into a hay supply at one of the company barns in the center of Lincoln. Immediately, the fire ran

Coming dowm the tracks along the Wilderness Trail is the East Branch & Lincoln Railroad with a full load of timber.

The fire of May 13, 1907, left Main Street, which was most of Lincoln's business district, in ruins. This view, looking southwest, includes the sawmill on left.

out of control and before they could extinguish it, many homes had burned, including those of John and George Henry, as well as some of the company buildings in the center and east end of Lincoln." Shortly after that disaster, another general alarm fire roared out of control on the Franconia Branch. However, that fire was caused by a lightning strike high on the east side of Owl's Head.

One month later, Thomas Will described the results of the logging: "Again prophecy has become history. On August 10th, Forester Ayers of the Society for the Protection of New Hampshire Forests and Secretary Will of the American Forestry Association sat on Mount Lafayette and looked over some 25,000 acres clean cut by the J.E. Henry Co. The ground was thickly covered with branches, tops, and logs. They predicted that forest fires would soon sweep this region."

The August 19, 1907 issue of *Among the Clouds* (Aug.19, 1907) stated: "A forest fire was noticed from the summit of Mount Washington, Saturday in the valley between the Franconia and Twin ranges, or more exactly, to the east of Mounts Flume and Liberty and west of Bond and Guyot and not many miles from North Woodstock. Sunday night the volume of smoke had increased and this morning it rose in a great mass, wholly hiding Mount Moosilauke. Driven before the northwest wind the smoke had gone beyond Lake Winnipesaukee and lay over the valleys far toward the ocean; while some other current had carried a long streak of smoke towards Vermont. The destruction of timber must have been enormous."

Karl P. Harrington describes this fire in *Walks and Climbs in the White Mountains:* "From the peaks of the Franconia Range, the fire could be seen burning in various directions.

A forest fire sweeps through the upper Pemigewasset Valley in August 1907. The area was identified as Camp No. 12, owned by the lumbering company of J.E. Henry & Sons.

Once the logs reached this sawmill in Lincoln, they were pulled out of the river for cutting.

At both ends of Owl's Head the thick smoke arose, and brands were carried across the intervening valley to the slopes of Mount Bond, and some of the camps were threatened with speedy ruin. A large force of men was sent out to fight the fire, with only moderate success; and many days passed before rain and the dying of the winds ended the devastation."

On August 27, 1907, the *Boston Post* ran an editorial that stated, in part, "In the once virgin and beautiful White Mountain region it is happening as predicted. Following the lumbermen comes the fire, and it is the end of forest beauty for not less than a generation and perhaps forever . . . Survey from Mount Lafayette shows Mount Bond to be swept clean, the easterly slope of Mount Garfield burned over, and the southerly slope of Mount Guyot fiercely burning with flames eating up Mount Lafayette."

James E. Henry retired from his position with the company a year later, just one year before the company's paper mill at Lincoln burned in 1909. He died on April 19, 1912, leaving his mark on the mountain landscape. However, as C. Francis Belcher, in his *Logging Railroads of the White Mountains* (1980), suggests, "Do not judge Henry or his methods unfairly. In 1900 the infant science of forestry knew few methods. It took the Henrys of the day to develop the science of forestry of the present, even if by a negative example. Despite his critics, Henry and his lumbering were as much a part of that era as the asphalt jungle and the real estate sprawl are of today's."

Transaction

On August 30, 1917, one of the highest priced real estate sales in New Hampshire of that

Indian Head, a profile resembling a Native American, projects from a rocky ledge on Mount Pemigewasset (2,557 feet) in the town of Lincoln.

time was transacted. The Henry company sold to the Parker-Young Company the East Branch & Lincoln Railroad, 100,000 acres of woodland, 150 homes, three mills—a sulfite, a ground-wood, and a paper mill—a steam plant, a distribution system, a hotel, a hospital, Livermore Falls water rights, camps, and icehouses. The problems besetting Parker-Young after the flood of 1927 and the Great Depression resulted in the sale of its East Branch timberlands to the U.S. government. On October 10, 1946, the company's assets were acquired by the Marcalus Manufacturing Company and then, in 1950, those same properties were bought by the Franconia Paper Corporation, which continued to operate the pulp and paper mills. The sawmill era came to an end, with the last log being sawed in June 1960.

Indian Head

On the south side of Pemigewasset Mountain in Lincoln is the mountain formation known as Indian Head. The mountainside's natural contours present a sharp profile resembling that of a Native American. This attraction lies is off the Daniel Webster Highway, where a 72-foot-high steel observation tower offers the best view of Indian Head. The tower was moved here from the town of Apthorp in the summer of 1921 so that observers could clearly see the profile across and above the forest. From this vantage point, the sharp outline stands out against the western horizon. This natural curiosity is somewhat less famed than the Old Man of the Mountain in the Franconia Notch.

Rev. Guy Roberts, in his *Indian Head, Its Debut and Legends* (1923), writes: "The attitude and expression of this profile is that of stoical repose, which in times of peace is characteristic of the Indian. The details of this profile are remarkably good, the forehead being retreating,

From the tower at Indian Head, visitors were able to get a good view of Mount Liberty (4,459 feet), as well as the Pemigewasset Valley to the south.

the nose large and prominent, the lower lip protruding, which even the eye and mouth are visible, excelling [the Old Man of the Mountain] in this respect. From the top of the forehead the mountain forest runs back suggestive of the Indian war-bonnet of trailing feathers, which in the autumn especially assumes the proper Indian colors of brown, red, yellow and green. Unlike "The Old Man of the Mountain" profile this one does not jut out abruptly, over hanging into space, but is in more of a retreating pose, gazing southward down over the beautiful Pemigewasset Valley."

In August 1922, Roberts ascended Indian Head and secured the following measurements: "The head being 98 feet from the top of the forehead to the bottom of the chin. The forehead itself being 17 feet high; the nose, 42 feet long; the upper lip, 23 feet wide, which leaves 16 feet for the chin. The Pemigewasset Mountain, on which the Indian Head is formed, is 2,563 feet in elevation, the top of the Head being 1,260 feet above the base of the observation tower."

An Indian raid occurred in this region of the White Mountains in 1812. According to Roberts, "The Pioneer settler of this region, David Guernsey, who migrated here in 1807,

This popular camping area, located at the base of Indian Head, included the 72-foot steel observation tower when this picture was taken c. the 1920s.

aided by other settlers built a two-story blockhouse of square hewed logs near the site of the present Indian Head souvenir store, for the defense of the settlers against Indian attacks. The upper story of this blockhouse projected 8 feet beyond the first, thus affording great advantage to those within it. In the fall of 1812, members of the Abenaki tribe incited by the English, besieged this place of refuge only to be vanquished by the sturdy settlers under the leadership of Mr. Guernsey. Later the tribe returned to Canada, where still later they were all exterminated excepting 12 persons only. This blockhouse stood until 1892, when it was torn down being in ruins. Leander Guernsey, great grandson of its builder and a nearby resident still, helped demolish the building, finding stone arrowheads imbedded in the logs, mute witnesses of the terrific contest of 80 years before."

Stephen Hanson, who lived and died about a mile south of Indian Head, told a traditional story of how Chief Pemigewasset used the ledge atop Mount Pemigewasset that now forms Indian Head as a lookout post when he feared the approach of the Algonquin tribe from the south. If he saw smoke down the valley it was a warning of danger, which he and his braves were quick to heed.

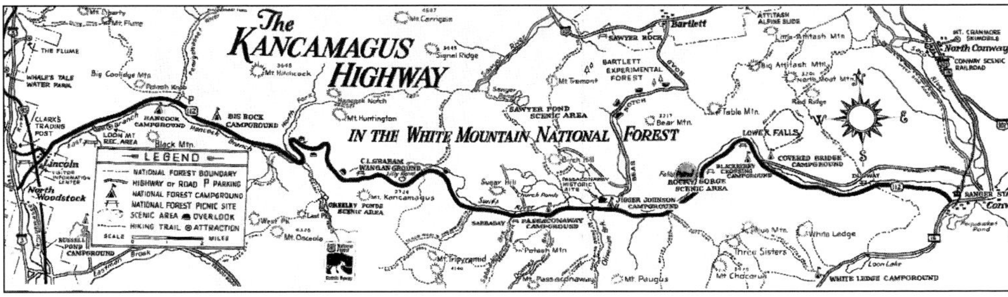

Since 1968, the Kancamagus Highway has been a vital link connecting the Pemigewasset Valley communities with the Conways, on the eastern slopes of the White Mountains. The Kancamagus is the only highway in northern New England that has been designated a National Scenic Byway.

The Kancamagus Highway

Starting in Lincoln at the Pemigewasset River, the scenic road known as the Kancamagus Highway (Route 112) runs 34.5 miles east to Conway. The route provides some of the most beautiful roadside views in the White Mountains and offers rich recreational opportunities. The Swift River runs alongside much of the route, and scenic areas have been designated by the National Forest Service, among them Rocky Gorge, Sawyer Pond, and Greeley Ponds. Markers are posted for trails, camping sites, and historic spots.

The road was named for an early chief of the Penacook Confederation, Kancamagus, who tried to keep peace between his people and the early white settlers. His efforts were in vain, resulting in war and bloodshed. During the early 1690s, the Penacook tribes scattered and Kancamagus and his people moved north to upper New Hampshire and Canada.

The first part of the route was laid out in 1837 as a Passaconaway town road. In the mid-1920s, a single-lane gravel road was constructed along the Swift River and, between 1933 and 1935, 11.3 miles of the east end, called Swift River Road, was upgraded and surfaced. Construction of a 7.6-mile section from Lincoln to Hancock Branch was begun in 1939. Construction and improvements continued over the next 20 years, until 1959, when the final 1.2-mile link was completed. The road was not completely paved until 1964, and it was not open to year-round travel until 1968.

Clark's Trading Post

Clark's was established in 1928 on Route 3 in Lincoln by Edward and Florence Clark for the purpose of raising and exhibiting Eskimo sled dogs. At that time, it was called Ed Clark's Eskimo Sled Dog Ranch; later, it became Clark's Trading Post. In 1930, the Clarks added bears to their dog ranch and, in 1949, the family introduced the bear show. Four generations of Clarks have kept the trading post going. Today, along with the bear performances, Clark's offers a museum, a replica of an old garage, small shops, and a 30-minute ride on the White Mountain Central Railroad, which debuted in 1958.

Ed Clark's Eskimo Dog Ranch opened in 1928 for the purpose of raising and exhibiting Eskimo sled dogs.

Located one mile north of North Woodstock, Clark's Trading Post, is a seasonal attraction that has grown over the years.

Loon Mountain

Off the Kancamagus Highway in Lincoln is Loon Mountain (3,065 feet), a former logging community that has been transformed into a resort. In the winter months, it offers prime skiing; in the warmer months, it provides gondola and train rides, hiking and biking trails, and shops and restaurants. Views from the summit of Loon Mountain include villages nestled below, the valley of the Pemigewasset River off to the south, Mount Moosilauke rising in the west, Franconia Notch and Loon Pond to the north, and the valley of the Three Rivers to the east.

Sherman Adams

The man who was the "driving force" behind the development of the Loon Mountain Ski Area was Sherman Adams, according to Dr. Richard M. Chisholm of Plymouth State College. Adams (1899–1986) was an avid outdoorsman and professional logger for 25 years before he began his 17-year political career as governor of New Hampshire and as chief aide to Pres. Dwight D. Eisenhower. Adams saw the opportunity to change Loon from a logging town into a White Mountain tourist attraction and he and seized it.

Attending Dartmouth College in Hanover from 1916 to 1920, Adams was strongly interested in mountaineering and skiing. As trail leader for the Dartmouth Outing Club, he organized hiking, climbing, and skiing trips. He was one of a group of five to make the first winter ascent of the Tuckerman Ravine headwall in 1917. To prove that all of the Dartmouth Outing Club cabins were "within a day's hike of Hanover," he, William P. Fowler, and other friends hiked in one day from Skyline Cabin, north of Littleton, to Dartmouth, a distance of 83 miles. Fowler recalls Adams as "slender, wiry, with muscles of steel . . . a driver, sparing neither himself nor companions. Of him alone will I admit that I have seen times when he could walk me ragged. He snapped along for mile after mile, his whole frame shaking from his machinelike muscle-action."

Adams was involved in the timber industry for a quarter of century and was known as "that well-known lumberman." He started as a recruiter for logging companies, rounding up men from Boston for operations in northern New England. In August 1923, he married Rachel White and moved to Lincoln, which remained his real home for the rest of his life. During his career as a logger, Adams walked every trail and traversed every square mile of the hills east of Lincoln. Even in the late 1960s he remained, as Phil Gravink said, "an intense hiker. Going up the hill, he would hike almost any of his guests into the ground within the first half mile. At times he would even go on and leave them, and say, 'I haven't got all day to dawdle. I'll see you at the top.'" At the time, Adams was approaching 70. In the winter of 1964, he spent a good many days searching for an ideal slope for his ski area. "I took my snowshoes and went out to look for a mountain," Adams wrote. "All alone, one day in February, I crossed the East Branch and set out for the top of Loon Mountain . . . This was it"—the site was in the town of Lincoln, two miles from his home of more than four decades, in the heart of the once thriving timber region. Having found the place, he consulted the experts and had them construct the ski area. During much of the construction, Adams was on the hill. "Mr. Adams would climb that mountain three times a day," said Rita Rand, his first secretary. Roland Bourassa, his lieutenant, agreed: "When you were working on the mountain, you could expect him to show up at any time and any place." For his ski trails he took names from the old logging days to perpetuate the memory of the timber industry that was being erased by the burgeoning tourist, skiing, and second-home industries. Later, as guests from those earlier times returned to visit the slopes, a surprising number of them spoke to staff at the resort of having "walked the hills with Sherman Adams."

This view of Mount Moosilauke was taken from the summit of Loon Mountain.

A Perspective

The following perspective of Lincoln appeared in the *Pycolog* on October 23, 1946. It was written by Martin A. Brown. "I sincerely hope that Lincoln, the community, can go on forever; that from year to year it will become a place in which to live and enjoy living. I know of few communities where the people get more out of life and out of their association with one another; as in all things, we still should start each day with a desire and determination to do more and better things."

From Mount Hancock (4,403 feet), the Lincoln wilderness spreads out toward the Presidential Mountain Range on the horizon.

Eight
Franconia Notch

The way north on Route 3 leads into southern end of Franconia Notch, which is about six miles in length. The notch is a deep cut in the Pemigewasset wilderness, with the mountains of the Franconia Range on the east and those of the Kinsman Range on the west, all draining into the East Branch of the Pemigewasset River. The mountains are high and close enough to accentuate the wildness of the scene but distant enough to give perspective. Occasionally visible are Mounts Lafayette (5,249 feet), Lincoln (5,108 feet), and Liberty (4,460 feet). The conspicuous solid rock wall is Cannon (Profile) Mountain (4,100 feet). In this area are natural wonders such as the Flume, the Pool, the Basin, the Old Man of the Mountain profile, and Echo and Lonesome Lakes.

Franconia Notch is an impressive example of the results of glacial action. The preglacial stream valley was positioned much as it is today; however, the Pemigewasset River was not as deep and the slopes were much rounder. The floor of the original valley was worn down, perhaps by several hundred feet, and the ice moving through the notch steepened the mountainsides, producing high walls such those at Eagle Cliff and Cannon Mountain.

Some travelers who pass through Franconia notch see mainly its quiet beauty and feel a sense of deep repose. They leave refreshed, and tranquil, and composed. Others such Swedish novelist Fredericka Bremer find it "playful" and "fantastic," even more enchanting than the famous regions of Dalecarlia and Norsland in her country. She wrote, "This scenery here is more picturesque, more playful and fantastic, has more cheerful diversity, and the affluence of wood and the beautiful foliage in the valleys is extraordinary: you walk or drive continually between the most lovely wild hedges of hazel, elm, sumach, sugar maple, yellow birch, fir trees, pines, and many other trees and shrubs, and on all sides is heard the singing and roaring of the mountain streams, clear as silver, through the passes of the hills." Thomas Starr King, who explored and wrote about the area, declared that Franconia Notch "contains more objects of interest to the mass of travelers than any other region of equal extent with the compass of the usual White Mountain tour."

The Road

The way through Franconia Notch was an old Native American trail, which eventually came to be called the Franconia Road. After Franconia Township was granted in 1764, the first settlers arrived on foot, horseback, and oxcart, following the trail through a virgin wilderness, said to be so thick that few views of the mountains could be seen. As more settlers arrived, the blazed trail became a rough wagon route that, by 1800, had become the major link with other parts of New England. Even settlers living to the north of the area traveled through Franconia Notch to trade their wilderness crops for salt, sugar, flour, gunpowder, tools, and spices in the markets of Portsmouth and Boston.

In 1805, the state hired Enoch Colby to lay out a road between Franconia and Peeling (now Woodstock) and Colby in turn hired Nathaniel Hall of Thornton. In 1813, the rough

Early travelers tour Franconia Notch by stagecoach.

A carful of people motor through Franconia Notch in the 1920s. In the background is the old Lafayette House, which later became a dormitory and garage for the Profile House. In later years as automobile traffic increased, a paved highway became a necessity to accommodate the traveling public.

survey line was cleared of trees, stumps, and rocks, and the first road was constructed. At first it was a toll road, called the Pemigeweasset Turnpike. "A man on horseback paid one cent per mile, a two-wheel or cart, one and a half cents per mile, a drove of ten cattle, two cents per mile. During the winter, a man and a one-horse sled paid two cents per mile. Mail was being carried by horseback at the rate of six cents per mile, plus postage."

After word of the Old Man of the Mountain and other natural wonders of the region reached the outside world, visitors arrived. By the mid-1800s, hotels had been established and the road had been somewhat improved. Tourists viewed Franconia Notch from stagecoaches that charged first-class passengers $7. Second-class passengers, who had to get out and walk up the hills, paid $3. Third-class passengers, who had to get out and push the coach up the hills, paid $1.50. When the horse and carriage era arrived, major improvements were made to the roadway, with tar replacing gravel in the mid-1920s and the first snowplow used in 1927. Enoch Colby's road had come of age.

This aerial view shows the massive granite ledge where the Old Man of the Mountain (see Chapter 10) is located, along with Profile and Echo Lakes.

Your Dollar Will Stop This

FIFTEEN or twenty miles this side of Fabyans and Bretton Woods, the White Mountain tourist who has motored northward over the Daniel Webster Highway comes upon an enchanting little tarn known as Profile Lake, or "The Old Man's Washbowl." Close at hand is a signpost marking the spot which commands the finest view of the Profile, or "Old Man of the Mountains." The Profile is formed by granite ledges on the upper cliffs of Mt. Cannon, or Profile. The face, which looks toward the southeast, is 80 feet in height and 1200 feet above the lake. It was discovered in 1805 by two men who were working on the Notch road. They were washing their hands in the lake and happened to glance up and see the Profile.

The 6,000 acres of woodland which in part make up the realm of the Great Stone Face are seriously threatened by the lumberman and his axe. Unless $82,800 can be collected in One Dollar gifts before March 1, 1928, campers and tourists may expect to see Franconia Notch given over to saw mills. All who love nature and find inspiration in the mountains will be glad to co-operate in saving this world-famous scenic shrine.

Boston American Dec. 27, 1927

Published in the December 27, 1927 edition of the Boston American, this notice seeks $82,800 in contributions to preserve the "6,000 acres of woodland" that are "seriously threatened by the lumberman and his axe."

In September 1928, Franconia Notch State Park was dedicated as a memorial to "the men and women of New Hampshire who served the nation in times of war." The dedication plaque mentions that the park was acquired with funds appropriated by the legislature and with donations from 15,000 contributors.

Franconia Notch State Park

The 1923 fire that destroyed the Profile House in Franconia was the event that aroused public demand for the state to purchase and preserve Franconia Notch. The establishment of the Franconia Notch State Park was authorized in 1925 by a legislative act, which appropriated $200,000 for that purpose. The Society for Protection of New Hampshire Forests (formed earlier to protect land in the White Mountains from private logging operations, landslides, and fire) raised a similar amount, using a bequest of $100,000 from James J. Storrow of Boston. The state acquired title to more than 5,000 acres, including Cannon Mountain, Echo Lake, Profile Lake, Lonesome Lake, and the Basin. The Society for Protection of New Hampshire Forests took title to the Flume and the adjacent 1,000 acres, agreeing to transfer title to the state in 1948. The dedication of the park was held on September 15, 1928. The following is an excerpt from the dedication ceremony:

> We have come together today for a unique and memorable occasion. We are about to dedicate a great open air Park to posterity. New Hampshire has set her seal upon a Notch of lofty grandeur and wild beauty, upon whose riven side stands out this age old monument, the Old Man of the Mountain, whose benign face has looked down upon every epoch of our history with inspiration and blessing. . . .
>
> New Hampshire has been fortunate at all times in her choice of leaders, but never more so than when through the skillful guidance of Governor John G. Winant the bill was passed in the legislature of 1925 to purchase this Notch. To Governor Winant and the legislature of 1925 great credit is due for their vision and generosity.

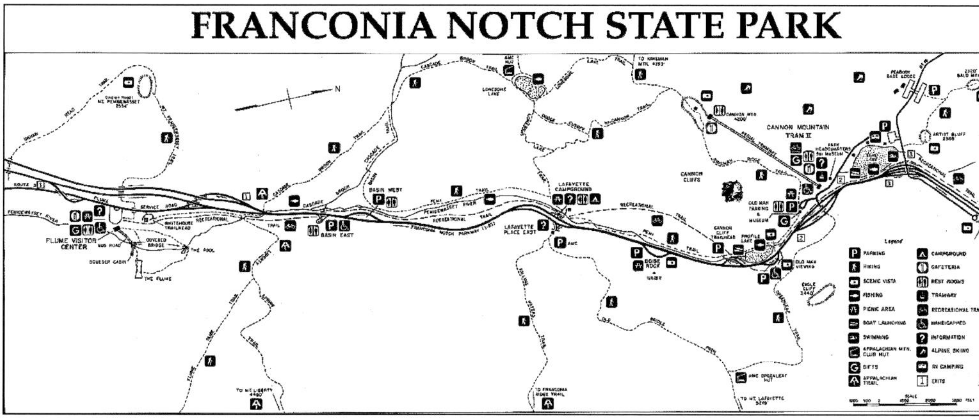

This 1968 map shows Franconia Notch State Park with the approved Franconia Parkway, Interstate 93. Located in the heart of the White Mountains, Franconia Notch extends from the Flume at the south end to Echo Lake to the north end. The eight-mile-long parkway winds between the peaks of the Kinsman and Franconia Mountain Ranges.

> For 27 years a band called the Society for Protection of New Hampshire Forests has carried on in New Hampshire, striving to save the scenic forests and acquire parks and playgrounds for our people. To their former endeavors we already owe such splendid contributions as Crawford Notch, Monadnock Mountain, Lost River, Sunapee Lake, Waterville, and a score of smaller reservations, and to these now will be added Profile Notch. To them the State owes a lasting debt of gratitude. Especially to their devoted manager, Mr. Philip W. Ayres, who first conceived the idea of this purchase, and to their honored President, Mr. Allen Hollis, whose unremitting labor and tireless pursuance of negotiations carried the purchase through to a conclusion. . . .
>
> —W.R. Brown
> Chairman, State Forestry Commission

Franconia Notch Parkway

As traffic increased, so did the demand for better roads. In 1944–1945, the New Hampshire Department of Public Works and Highways in cooperation with the then Bureau of Public Roads recommended Franconia Notch-Interstate 93. Heavy construction and blasting through the notch caused great concern among the keepers of the profile on Cannon Mountain, known as the Old Man of the Mountain. They feared that the vibrations might cause rocks to move. In 1954, at the state's request, University of New Hampshire experts conducted a geological study. The study determined that the crevice across the top of the head of the Old Man of the Mountain had widened by three quarters of an inch since it had been measured by Edward H. Geddes in 1937. The section that had moved was estimated to weigh in excess of 300 tons. Officials, therefore, designed and installed four large turnbuckles, to fasten down of a number of loose boulders, and sealed of several small cracks with epoxy. In addition, the constructed a sluiceway some distance in back of the head, and a wire fiberglass cloth-covered canopy to cover the large crevice.

After further study and public input, the state approved Franconia Notch as the location for Interstate 93 in 1966 and design work began in 1969. However, concern for the safety of the Old Man of the Mountain delayed the highway project. More ground-vibration studies were approved in January 1968, with the state and federal governments sharing the costs. Those studies concluded that regardless of road work, the struggle to save the stone formation may be futile. "Natural forces are at work against 'The Old Man' and I'm afraid that they will eventually emerge victorious," said state materials and research engineer Paul S. Otis.

In the end, the Cotton Amendment authorized the U.S. secretary of transportation, "upon application of the Governor of the State, to approve construction of that section of Interstate Route 93, from [the] interchange with State Route 3A in North Woodstock . . . to . . . an interchange with U.S. Route 3 in Franconia . . . approximately twelve miles in length, as a parkway type highway to geometric and construction standards (whether or not in accordance with section 109 (b), which the Secretary determines are necessary for the safety of the traveling public, for the protection of the environment, and for the preservation of the park-like and historic character of the Franconia Notch area adjacent to the highway."

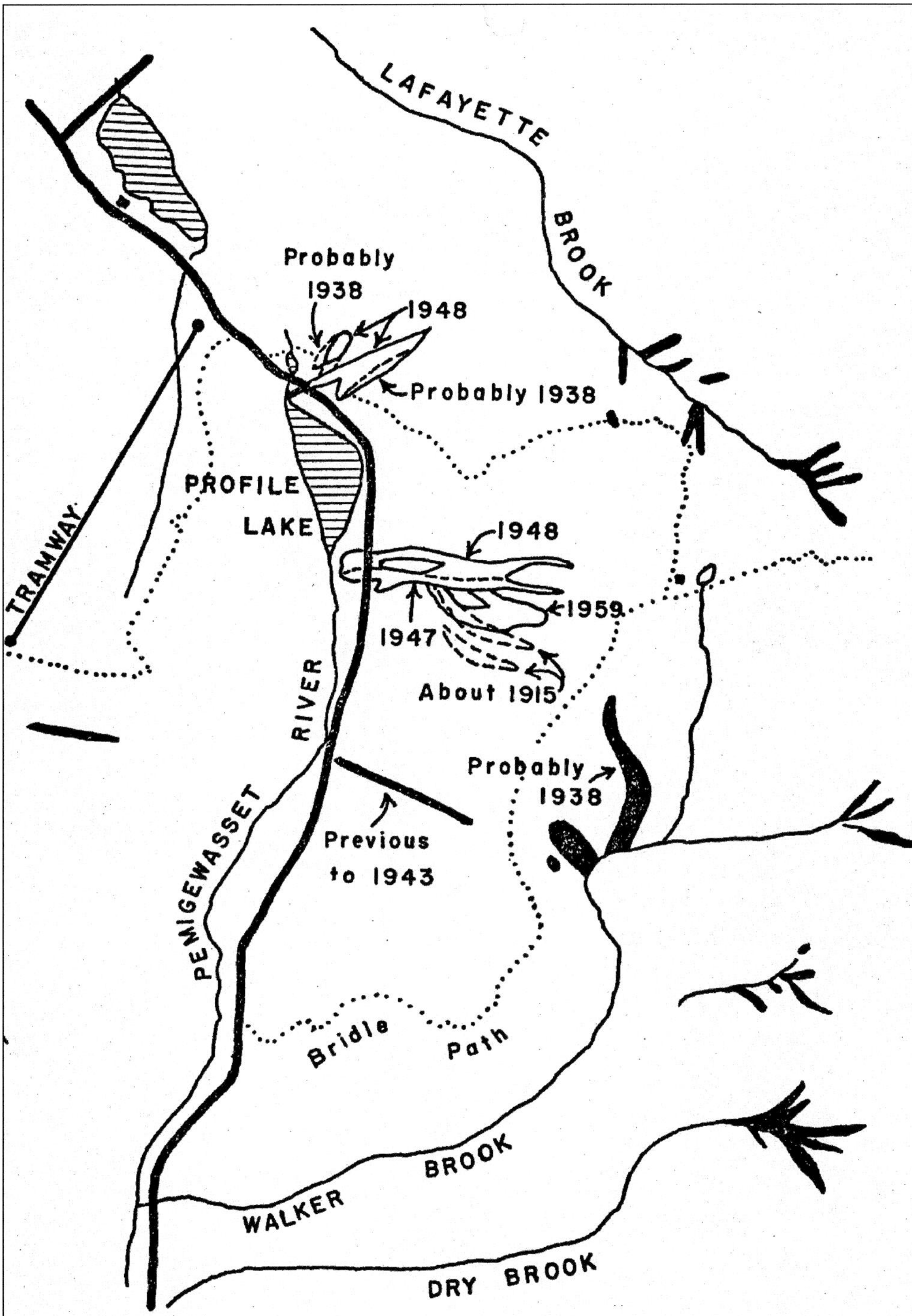

Past landslides, marked with arrows and dates, indicate points of greatest danger to the roadway.

Harvard Falls

Some two miles off Route 3 near Mount Pemigewasset the outlet of Bog Pond empties over an 80-foot cliff, creating Harvard Falls. The falls are reached by a faint trail that crosses a high ridge and leads down into the valley of the Harvard Brook, a dark colored stream with woody water filled with large trout. The best viewing point is about 200 feet below, on the left bank, where the white column of water is seen over its deep basin and recessed between jagged and dark-colored cliffs of coarse granite. The falls include cascades above and below, and a beautiful basin called the Mirror near the upper ledge. The cliffs above the falls offer a splendid view down the Pemigewasset Valley. Harvard Falls were discovered and christened in 1858, although a party of students claimed to have found and named them earlier. Due to their isolated forest location, the falls are visited rather rarely. Even though the hike is difficult, the forests on the ascent afford rich woodland scenery, diversified by the ledges and the rushing brook.

The Flume

On the western side of Mount Flume is a natural gorge known as the Flume. The geological history of the Flume is briefly told in signs at important points. The granite of the rocks was formed many millions of years ago; later a dark-colored molten lava was pushed up through the cracks and crevices. Posted signs indicate these lava seams. The cooling lava solidified into dikes, and the principal one was eroded until the flume-gorge was formed. The frosts of thousands of years, and the rushing of water have widened the canyon.

In June 1807, pioneer settlers David and Jess Guernsey and their family migrated from Plymouth, bringing all their possessions with them on the backs of six horses. They came to the wilderness, over what was then a simple trail, and settled at the present Indian Head. Legend has it that Jess Guernsey, at 93 years old, was in remarkably good health and was excellent at fishing. In 1808, she wandered into the wilderness and happened upon a remarkable phenomenon: the Flume Gorge. She realized its importance and immediately reported it to her husband. Word passed quickly, and the Flume became a natural curiosity. A verse from one of Hibbard's poems well describes this wonder:

> And farther down from Guernsey's lone abode,
> By a rude footpath climb the mountain side,
> Leaving below the travelers' winding road,
> To where the cleft hill yawns abrupt and wide,
> As tho some earthquake did its mass divide
> In olden time; there view the Rocky Flume,
> Tremendous chasm! rising side by side,
> The rocks abrupt wall in the long, high room,
> Echoing the wild stream's roar, and dark with vapory
> gloom.

These falls are located on Harvard Brook.

This scene shows a busy day c. 1920 at the Flume Visitor Center.

The 800-foot-long canyon varies in width from 12 to 20 feet, and its walls of Conway granite rise from 70 to 90 feet in height. In places its perpendicular walls appear uniform, as if they had been put up by human hands. At the upper the walls are lower, the floor is higher, and the gorge widens. At various points trees arcade the chasm, and birches, lichens, and vines are grow from crevices in the rock. Running between these walls is Flume Brook, which has its sources on Mounts Flume and Liberty.

The Lost Boulder of the Flume

The walkway crosses and recrosses the stream on small bridges. Near the upper end of the chasm, about six feet below the upper-level platform, a huge boulder was for centuries lodged between the walls about 12 feet up. The boulder was egg shaped, about 10 feet wide and 12 feet long. On June 20, 1883, a cloudburst on Mount Liberty started a landslide of earth and trees—in one place half a mile wide—a large part of which came sweeping down the Flume. In the process the landslide tore the boulder from its suspended position. Also torn off in the landslide was the large inward-leaning wall where the boulder had once hung. This widened the chasm at what had been the narrowest part to its present width of approximately 16 feet.

No one has been able to determine for sure where the boulder ended up. Some claim that a huge rock lying near the mouth of the Flume is the lost boulder. This rock is located 18 yards from the end of the boardwalk above the footbridge, at nearly right angles to it, across the stream in the edge of the bushes. Postcard photographs showing it as the lost boulder can be found in many souvenir shops. However, the huge rock does not conform to the egg shape of the lost boulder. Moreover, the late J.R. Elliott, proprietor of the Flume at the time the Boulder came tumbling down, is on record as being "firmly convinced that the right stone has never been found."

This is the lower end of the Flume, the first view of the gorge that visitors see.

Tourists pose in the gorge c. 1880. Behind them, suspended high between the walls of the Flume, is the famous Boulder.

In this view of the Flume, the Boulder can be seen wedged between the walls (upper left). The huge egg-shaped rock was washed away during a flood in June 1883.

Some 40 feet deep, the Pool is a granite basin filled with water that appears almost black. It is approximately 150 feet in diameter and is surrounded by high cliffs.

Avalanche Falls and the Pool

At the upper end of the Flume, Avalanche Falls tumble down a series of granite steps. The path crosses the falls below a wide basin and returns by an equally impressive route along the Rim Path. To the right on the Flume Slide Trail, Mount Flume (4,327 feet) rises. Half-moon in shape, the summit has a scattered growth of low spruce and offers an extensive panorama of the Franconia area, the Pemigewasset wilderness to the east, and the far-extending lowlands.

The Rim Pool Path leads to Liberty Gorge, a beautiful 70-foot cascade, and then down a series of steps to a stygian body of water known as the Pool. The Pemigewasset falls in a cascade over a mass of rocks into this 150-foot-diameter, 40-foot-deep granite basin, a geological pothole filled with water that is looks almost black. High surrounding cliffs contribute to the eeriness of the scene.

The mighty cascade of water at the upper end of the Flume is known as Avalanche Falls.

Built in 1872 on the same site as the First Flume House, the second Flume House had accommodations for 150 guests and in its time was a mecca for tourists.

The First Flume House

Visitors began coming to stay in the area as early as 1835. As their numbers increased, new hotels were built to accommodate them. One of the first hotels was the Flume House, built *c.* 1847 in a beautiful location not far from the Flume and other natural wonders. Until 1871, it offered accommodations for 100 to 150 guests. From the south veranda, guests looked down the Pemigewasset Valley. To the north they viewed the shape formed by the Franconia Mountains Range that is known as Washington Lying in State: Mount Liberty outlines Washington's upturned face, with the highest ledge as his nose; the ridges running to the north form his body and limbs. Thomas Starr King, in his book *The White Hills,* describes the outlook from the Flume Hotel: "The view from The Flume House itself is a perpetual refreshment, and one need not seek by hard climbing or wandering for any increased temptation to contentment."

The Second Flume House

After the first Flume House burned in 1871, the second was constructed and completed in 1872. According to the 1902 *Tourists' Guide-Book for the State of New Hampshire,* "The house is conducted in a most liberal and pleasing manner, and is maintained by a patronage of the highest order, consisting largely of families who spend the entire season under its hospitable roof, while it still retains its old charm each year in dining thousands of summer tourists from

Shown c. 1921 is the Flume Tea House, the former site of the renowned Flume House.

every section known in the White Mountains - coming, as they do, to visit that 'Miracle of Nature,' the Flume. Pleasant drives over well-kept roads may be enjoyed to all points of interest in the Franconia Notch, Bethlehem, Sugar Hill, or down the Pemigewasset Valley, East Branch road, Moosilauke Basin road, to Breezy Point." On June 27, 1918, the second Flume House was destroyed by fire; it was never rebuilt due to the economic uncertainty of the time. However, the Flume Tea House was opened at the site in later years.

The Cascades

A short way north on Route 3 from the Flume, the small Whitehouse Bridge passes over the Pemigewasset River. The bridge was named for a large white house that stood on the nearby clearing, in which lived the owner of a lumber mill. Remains of the dam can be seen in the riverbed. Off to left at the bridge is the Cascade Trail, leading to the Cascades, on Cascade Brook, a small tributary of the Pemigewasset. The lower section of the Cascades is a succession of sloping flat granite ledges, which in some places exceed 100 feet in width. From this vantage point are fine views of Eagle Cliff and the valley lying to the northeast. The Cascade Trail eventually unites with the Fishin Jimmy Trail, named after Annie Trumbull Slosson's story of Jimmy, an old fisherman. Off to the right at Whitehouse Bridge, the Whitehouse-Liberty Spring Trail leads to Mount Liberty (4,460 feet).

Formed by the continuous action of water and rocks streaming into it, the Basin is about 15 feet deep and 30 to 40 feet wide.

The Basin

At the side Route 3, north of the Whitehouse Bridge, is a deep granite hollow known as the Basin. Over a geological span of time, this pothole has sunk to a depth of 15 feet and widened to a diameter of 30 to 40 feet. The Basin catches the waters of the Pemigewasset as they flow down from Profile Lake, over a low rocky ledge. Through the transparent water, the pure bed of the basin can be distinctly seen. On one side the rocks jut over the depths, forming a dam for the flowing stream and producing an exquisite waterfall. In season, the embankment surrounding the Basin is covered with green mosses and sweet flowers. Just below here is the mouth of Cascade Brook, which, by many, is considered to be the finest brook in America for scenery and small trout. About a mile up a labyrinthine path are the brilliant Tunnel Falls, and another half mile up are the rarely visited but very attractive Island Falls, which are three miles below Lonesome Lake.

William Oake's *Scenery of the White Mountains* describes the Basin:

> The bottom is strewn with rocks, and is apparently level. Its sides and margin are beautifully regular and very smooth; and the high bank of the same solid, continuous, gray granite is elegantly arched beneath, and stained with dark purple.
>
> In a hot day in summer, the pure, clear, and cold waters below, foaming and sparkling in their clean granite bowl, are delightful and refreshing to the eye and imagination. The perpendicular cascade, white with foam, falls gracefully over its brink from the rocky bed of the river above, and striking the water of the basin nearly parallel to its side, gives the whole a strong revolving motion. Branches of trees thrown into the

This c. 1933 view shows the peaks of the Franconia Range from Lonesome Lake.

whirlpool are carried round many times before they are discharged, being alternately drawn to the bottom, and brought again to the top. It would probably be a dangerous bathing-place for a weak swimmer, and its steep and slippery borders are not very safe for careless visitors.

In the hollow in the rocky bed of a rapid stream, where the waters form a whirlpool, a few rocks are accidentally lodged, and carried around by the revolving water, gradually grinding and wearing a round, smooth cavity, into which, as it enlarges, rocks of greater size and brought by the freshets. The process goes on until a wide and often very deep excavation is formed, which in places where the river has shifted its course are sometimes seen as deep pits, like wells, in the dry ground.

Lafayette Place

A short distance north from the Basin is Lafayette Place, the site of a small tavern built in 1835 and of the Mount Lafayette House, built in the late 1850s and destroyed by fire in 1861. To the left and across a bridge is the Lafayette Place Campground, with facilities for camping. Visible from Lafayette Place on the right is the Great Elephant, a formation on Eagle Cliff that resembles a recumbent pachyderm. According to the *American Guide Series of New Hampshire,* the elephant's trunk is "thrown out before him, his hind foot on the ground, while his haunch is thrown high in the air." A white spot in the cliff represents the eye.

Lonesome Lake.

A trail from Lafayette Place leads to Lonesome Lake. This small body of water, once known as Tamarack Pond, is located at an altitude of 2,743 feet on a ridge under one of the shoulders of Cannon Mountain. The ascent to the lake is well marked and easily accessible along a well-graded path. From the southwestern shore of the lake is a view of the rugged gray-white summits of Mount Lafayette and the Franconias above the adjacent forest, impressively indicating the depth of Franconia Notch. The immense solitude of the lake, ringed by heavy forest, imparts at once the feeling of the entire region, and accents the remoteness that gives the lake its name.

Mount Lafayette

Once called the Great Haystack (as on Carrigan's map of 1816), Mount Lafayette (5,249 feet) was renamed *c.* 1825 for the Marquis de Lafayette in gratitude for his assistance in the War of Independence. Located at the northern end of the wall in the Franconia Range that flanks the Pemigewasset River on the east, Lafayette is the second highest mountain in the region, after Mount Washington. Its summit affords a panoramic view of Franconia Notch, down the valley to Plymouth, southeast to the Sandwich Mountain Range, north to Mount Washington and the Canadian hills, and west to the Green Mountains. Closer views include the scarred sides Cannon Mountain across the notch, and the peak of Mount Lincoln (5, 089 feet) immediately to the south. Three trails lead to the summit: the four-mile Greenleaf Trail, a good three-and-a-half-hour hike from the site of the former Profile House; the Franconia Ridge from the south; and the Garfield Trail from the northeast.

The Greenleaf Trail

The Greenleaf Trail, named for Col. C.H. Greenleaf, leads east into the woods, descending gently until it crosses a brook, where the ascent begins by easy stages up the zigzag paths of Eagle Cliff. The path continues under the frowning bulk of Eagle Cliff and affords not only a glimpse of the Old Man of the Mountain but also some excellent views of Franconia Notch. In the configuration of the land, Eagle Cliff stands out from Lafayette with a gorge between that has interesting rock formations and caves. The trail moves eastward through the pass, over a level stretch, and on to the steep slope on the northwest flank of the mountain. Loose stones and wet weather pose hazards along this stretch. A mile above the pass, there is a spring 10 ten yards to the left of the trail. Half a mile farther up, the trail nears one of the sources of the Ammonoosuc River, which roars from the depth of a chasm 1,000 feet below. Soon, the surroundings begin to show the severity of the climate: the timberline grows less visible, the stunted spruce and thin birch are replaced by hardier vegetation. The trail rises above the spur that reaches over the notch and the carriage road that passes through it. The Pemigewasset Valley stretches out below. The summit of Cannon Mountain looks like a man's face covered with scabs while Lonesome Lake, held snugly below, looks like a child of the wilderness. The round-topped Mount Moosilauke rises in the southwest, concealing the Connecticut Valley. On one of the mountain's most inaccessible points is a strange looking stone. Those who discovered it named it the Altar because of its resemblance to old runic remains of a similar character.

At the last cliff below the crown of the peak, a small spring seeps. A thin ridge slopes off abruptly into wide chasms. Along it runs a peculiar narrow indention, said to have been caused by the feet of many passing animals. Above, the peak is bare except for the Greenland sandwort growing in the spaces between the rocks. Ridges extend from its north and south

Ascending Mount Lafayette, these hikers and horseback riders enjoy a leisurely afternoon on the trail near Greenleaf Pond.

Mount Lafayette (5,289 feet) is the highest of the Franconia peaks. In the valley is Echo Lake.

sides, with the north ridge stretching a half a mile to a subordinate peak of 5,075 feet in height. From the ravine on the right, the view is breathtaking. Mount Washington lies to the northeast, its great dome appearing over the nearer Twin Mountains; on very clear days, the houses and railroad tracks are visible in the valley below. Beyond Washington, the sharp point of Maine's Mount Katahdin rises. To the south, the valley of the Pemigewasset River opens all the way to Plymouth, a distance of 40 miles. In the southwest, Mounts Monadnock and Kearsarge break up the landscape. To the west, the rounded summits of Vermont's Green Mountains complete the circle.

The Garfield Trail

The Garfield Ridge Trail, to the north, travels the sharp crest which joins Lafayette to South Twin Mountain. Eventually, it winds to the northeast, descends to the timberline, and then gradually climbs, passing near Garfield Pond. A cutoff diverges to the left, leading to the

This photograph of Mount Lafayette was taken from the observation platform on Cannon Mountain.

outlet of the pond. At the pond's east end, a 150-yard side trail on the right leads to the old Garfield Pond shelter, a six-person hut built in 1917 for hikers by the Appalachian Mountain Club. The Garfield Trail then climbs the cone to within a few yards of the barren summit, which is reached by a short side path to the right. At this junction a direct trail to the highway forks to the left. Continuing, the Garfield Trail descends to the northeast in order to avoid some hazardous ledges directly east of the cone.

The White Mountains are full of trails and, as a rule, the trails are well marked with signs and kept in good repair by many different organizations. The most prominent organization is the Appalachian Mountain Club, which since 1876 has maintained hundreds of miles of trails and provides huts and shelters along these paths for the use of hikers. According to the *White Mountain Guide*, published by the Appalachian Mountain Club, "The Franconia Range ranks second among the ranges of the White Mountains only in elevation. Its sharp, narrow ridge contrasts strikingly with the broad massive Presidential Range."

Eagle Cliff on Mount Lafayette rises above Profile Lake.

Eagle Cliff (1,500 feet) is a precipitous foothill of Mount Lafayette. Below it is Profile Lake

Eagle Cliff and Boise Rock

Eagle Cliff, a gigantic spur separated from the crest of Mount Lafayette, rises straight up to a height of 3,466 feet across from Profile Lake. Its lofty crags stand out in full view from a point three fourths of a mile along the border of the lake. The cliff of jagged rock appears ready to topple from its place into widespread ruins below. It was named in 1858 by the Reverend Thomas Hill after he discovered an eagle's nest high on the cliff.

The legend of Boise Rock was handed down by Justus Conrad and other longtime residents of the region. Soon after the road was built through the Franconia Notch (1805), a noted character named Thomas Boise (Boyce) used to drive his team from Woodstock, where he lived, through the notch to Franconia. On one of his trips, he got caught in a severe snowstorm and had to stop. About three rods from the road, he found a large boulder that projected out several feet—perfect shelter from the storm. He killed his horse, skinned the animal, wrapped himself in the hide, and crawled under the rock for the night. He was found there the following day by men sent out to search for him. The animal hide was so frozen that it had to be cut open with a knife to Boise out. Boise was saved without having suffered greatly from exposure to the weather, and Boise Rock has been a landmark ever since. The boulder is located three fifths of a mile south of Profile Lake on the east side of Route 3, about 50 feet into the woods. It is a most unusual boulder, probably of glacial origin, resting wholly on top of the ground, with ample room under it to shelter a score of people. Looking something like a great war tank, it is 45 feet in length, 35 feet in width, and from 3 to 14 feet in thickness.

The Lafayette House in Franconia Notch is captured in this lithograph of a drawing by artist I. Sprague.

The Lafayette House

The Lafayette House (Gibb's Hotel) was built *c.* 1835 on a site southeast of the base of Cannon Mountain. Referred to originally as a "house of entertainment" (Knight's Tavern), it was one of the first hotels to serve visitors to the area. Owned and operated by Stephen C. Gibb and Maj. Joseph L. Gibb, the Lafayette House accommodated 50 guests.

Bryant F. Tollis Jr., in *The Grand Resort Hotels of the White Mountains,* writes, "During 1853, in conjunction with the construction of the first Profile House, the Lafayette House was moved across the Notch road to the rear of the new hotel. There it served as a "work room" and laundry until it was reconstructed and modernized for use as a dormitory for waitresses. . . . The Old Lafayette House underwent a final transformation in 1897 when it was converted into a new and attractive cottage for both male and female help. 'Lafayette Cottage' as it was renamed, had an added third story, altered fenestration and a new hipped roof similar to those of the New Profile House. When fire destroyed this grant resort hotel complex, on August 1923, the last remnants of the original Lafayette House were also lost."

The Profile & Franconia Notch Railroad was a narrow-gauge line that served only the Profile House. This short line went only as far as Bethlehem. Looming above the train station is Eagle Cliff (left), on Mount Lafayette.

The first Profile House spreads out on a level plateau in the midst of the hills. With its cottages and outbuildings, the hotel was the only settlement in this small area.

The First Profile House

The first Profile House was built in 1852–1853 with accommodations for 550 to 600 guests. It was a favorite retreat for New York clientele. Among its famous visitors were showman P.T. Barnum and financier Cornelius Vanderbilt. Enlarged over the years, the hotel became an extensive resort. With the large influx of tourists to the area, occasioned in part by the construction of a railroad between the Profile House and Bethlehem in 1881, the old hotel was regarded as inadequate and was torn down in 1905. It was immediately replaced by the second Profile House.

The Second Profile House

Advertisements for the new Profile House boasted that "it has long been noted as one of the leading summer resorts and favored with clientele of the highest order. Excursions by rail to all points in the White Mountains and return the same day. Parlor cars from New York and all New England cities; also accessible by coaches via Pemigewasset Valley; fine boating and fishing on Profile and Echo lakes. The analysis of Profile spring shows the purest of table water. A complete livery, with modern vehicles and trusty drivers. Beautiful drives and miles of mountain paths. The Profile golf links are well described by the following letter: 'I have yet to see the lovelier place, or one with more natural advantages for golf than the Profile House links in the White Mountains, and other clubs might well copy the way the Profile Club does in the manner of grass, trees, and piped greens, and with a good wet spring next year, it will be a course anybody will be delighted to play on.'"

The second Profile House operated from 1906 until it burned in 1922. Up to that time, Profile Lake was part of the hotel property and was kept thoroughly stocked with fish. Only the guests could use the lake or standing on its bank to view the Old Man of the Mountain.

In the main dining room at the Profile House, elegance and service were trademarks.

This c. 1900 view shows a country road approaching Cannon Mountain from the south.

The lake's location immediately below the famous profile offers the best vantage point. Note: The Old Man of the Mountain, the most photographed feature of the White Mountains, merits a chapter of its own and, thus, appears in chapter 10.

Cannon Mountain

Across the Franconia Notch Parkway from Eagle Cliff, rises Cannon Mountain (4,100 feet), or Profile Mountain as some refer to it. The former name derives from its supposed resemblance to a cannon; the latter from the profile of the Old Man of the Mountain, which is located on the southern extremity of its crest (see chapter 10). The mountain is a massive granite ledge with great areas of exposed rock area and a summit is covered with vegetation. Some parts are very precipitous, especially toward the souheast. It is separated from Mount Kinsman by a narrow and exceedingly rough valley. Cannon Mountain can be approached by way of the Kinsman Ridge Trail. The ascent is somewhat difficult, but view from the top reveals an enchanted pathway flanked by silvery streams, quiet forests, broad meadows, placid lakes, and clustering villages.

Visitors look northwest from the observation platform at the summit of Cannon Mountain c. 1940. A much larger structure serves the visitors of today.

The Tramway

In the spring of 1933, famous skier Alexander Bright had an idea. He developed the idea of constructing an aerial tramway in New Hampshire during his trip to Europe as a member of the U. S. Olympic Ski Team. Having noted the success of the tramway concept in Europe, he realized the potential it would have in the White Mountains. On one of New Hampshire's mountains, he wanted to build a tramway that would be not only a boon to skiers but also the means for summer tourists to ascend in safety to the summit. In 1938, his idea became reality with the opening of the Cannon Mountain Tramway, the first modern aerial passenger tramway on the North American continent.

Research into costs, returns, and possible sites, including Cannon and Gunstock Mountains, and Mounts Moosilauke and Lafayette, was undertaken in 1933. The following spring, a committee of three men appointed by Gov. John G. Winant selected Cannon, which had three main advantages: the high volume of tourists passing its base, the 11 square miles of state and federal property on the mountain, and the fact that construction could be completed without cutting any forests or marring the beauty of Franconia Notch. In June 17, 1937,

The Valley Station, or lower terminal, of the Cannon Mountain Tramway was built some 250 feet from the old roadway.

that the state passed a bill calling for $250,000 to finance the construction of the tramway. On August 26, 1937, the construction contract was awarded to the American Steel & Wire Company, and work started in September, with 150 working days allowed for completion. Men from a Civilian Conservation Corps in North Woodstock did some of the early work, constructing a parking area and some ski trails and practice areas.

The lower terminal, or Valley Station, was built 250 feet from the old highway; the upper terminal, or Mountain Station, approximately 300 feet from the summit and 200 feet from start of the Richard Taft Ski run and the Cannon Mountain Trail. The tramway started at an elevation of 1,981 feet and climbed to 3,993 feet—a difference in elevation of 2,012 feet and za horizontal distance of 5,000 feet. Between the landing points, the length of cable measured 5,410 feet. The cable extended over three towers, the first 106 feet high and the second and third 85 feet high, each giving a maximum clearance of about 40 feet over the treetops.

The tramway had two cars, each of which could hold 27 passengers and one attendant. As one car left the lower terminal, the other started its descent from the upper terminal, and they passed each other at the halfway point. The speed of the traction rope was 1,000 feet per minute. The running time per trip was 5 minutes, 28 seconds, and the time interval per trip, including station stops, was 7 minutes, 4 seconds. The hourly capacity in each direction was 225 passengers. The cars operated smoothly and almost noiselessly. They were controlled both from a master board at the Valley Station and by an operator in each car. The motive power consisted of alternating electric current, taken from the main transmission lines, and changed to direct current in the Valley Station. The direct-current motor operated traction cables and cars. In addition, a direct-current generator supplied power in case the main line

The ascending and descending tramway cars meet at the halfway point of the mile-long ride to the 4,200-foot summit of Cannon Mountain.

This view from below shows one of the tranway cars and the Mountain Station, or upper terminal, on Cannon Mountain.

service failed and, should both fail, a gasoline engine substituted a reserve source of operating power. When the cars neared either station they were automatically braked and brought to a smooth stop at the landing platform. Both upper and lower terminals were heated by steam and were operated year-round. Storms, even windstorms and snowstorms, did not hinder operations. In a snowstorm, the cars could run on automatic if visibility was poor. In a windstorm, the stabilizing device, the weight and tension of the cables, and limited car exposure area all helped limit swaying.

The tramway was a significant step in the development of the New Hampshire ski industry. Without this service, skiers could not possibly make more than two mountain descents in a single day. With the aid of the tramway, each car equipped with device for holding full quota of skis, the experienced downhill runner could complete a trip up and down the mountain in less than 20 minutes. The tramway also offered summer tourists the opportunity to ride safely over the trees to the summit for a full view of the region. From its opening in 1938 to its retirement in 1980, a period of 42 years, the first aerial tramway in North America took a total of 6,581,338 passengers on the 2.1-mile journey to the summit of Cannon Mountain. The second Cannon tramway, a Nuova Agudio, is one of the most technically advanced in the world. Dedicated on May 24, 1980, it has two cabins, each with a capacity of 80 passengers and one attendant, and ascends the 5,359-foot trip at a speed of 1,500 feet per minute. Its hourly passenger capacity is 1,540—770 in each direction—more than three times that of the original tramway.

The Cannon Mountain Tramway was the first passenger-carrying aerial one on the North American continent. At the base of the mountain are Echo Lake (left) and the parking lot for visitors. (right).

This view of the second Cannon Mountain Tramway was taken in 1980.

This busy scene is the boathouse at Echo Lake. The lake is named for the acoustic effect that is found here.

Echo Lake

Beyond the Cannon Mountain ski area off to the left of the Franconia Notch Parkway is Echo Lake. At an altitude of 1,931 feet, this lake is one of the reservoirs of the South Branch of the Ammonoosuc River, which eventually flows westerly toward the Connecticut River. From the center of the lake, a voice at regular volume will echo two or three times, but a shout will resound alarmingly. It is little wonder that Native Americans believed that the lake possessed an awful power. According to legend, a lone Indian who was being pursued by 100 armed warriors sought refuge here. He sent up his voice, and the echoing effect so startled his pursuers that they fled, believing that he had been reinforced by a band of friends too numerous to attack.

The echoing also made a summer tourist who ventured out on the lake think of armies: "Around us on all sides the clear water reflected back the high cliffs in all their beauty and

Looking out from atop Artist Bluff, Mount Lafayette rises on the right, Cannon Mountain ascends on the left, and Echo Lake lies in the valley below.

wildness. As we gave a loud 'hello' the mountain directly before us gave back the cry, like an army of men shouting from its summit. As that died away, the mountain behind us caught up the sound, and returned it like the shouting of an opposing army; and as that died out, the hills upon our right and left tossed back and forth the lessening shout, until it could be heard far off taking its flight. The several echoes are very distinct, and each commences as the preceding closes."

Who can say where Echo dwells?
In some mountain cavern methinks,
Where the white owl sits and blinks;
Or in deep, sequestered dells,
Where the foxlove hangs its bells
Echo dwells.
Echo!
Echo!

—Thomas Bailey Aldrich

Beyond Echo Lake are Artist Bluff (2,368 feet) and Bald Mountain (2,320 feet). A path north of the lake leads to Artist Bluff, which offers views that deserve to be painted on canvas. A climb up low and rocky Bald Mountain is also well worth the effort. Below are Franconia Notch, Profile Lake, and the valley to the south. Mount Lafayette towers in the southeast, and the Bethlehem hills rise in the north.

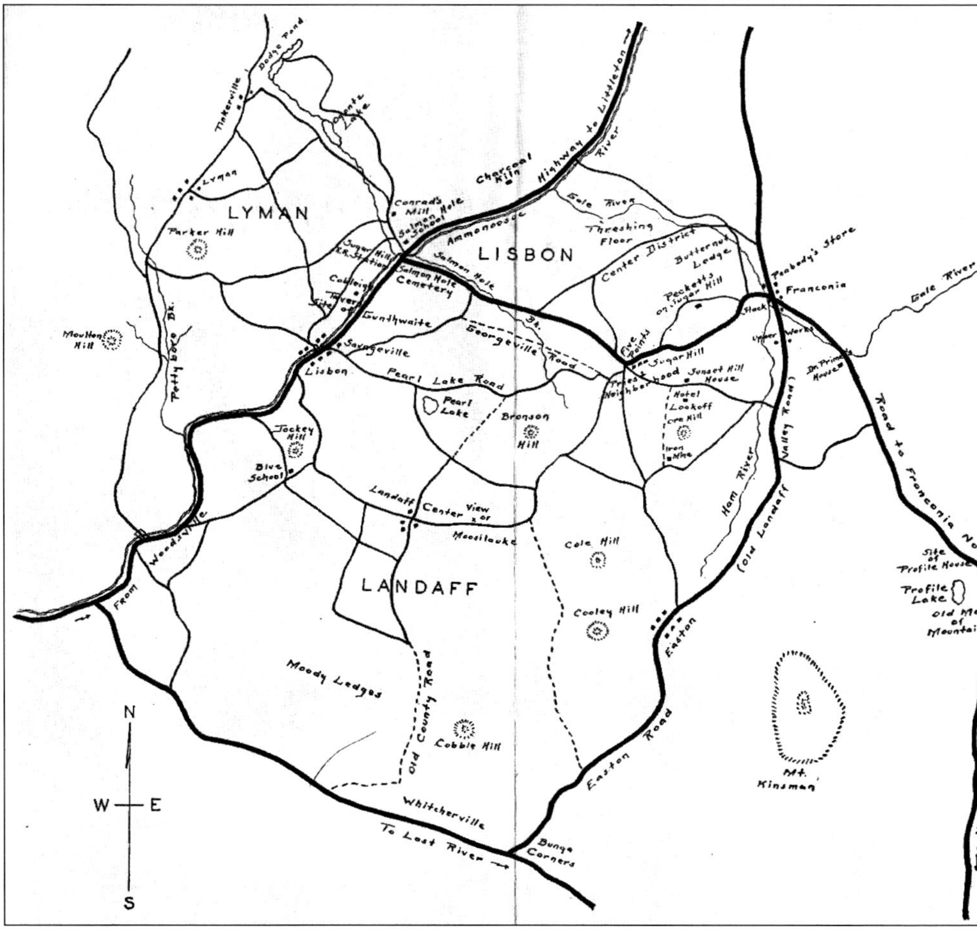

Shown on this map of Franconia are the hamlets of Landaff, Lisbon, and Lyman.

Nine
Franconia

From Echo Lake the high road winds down the steep mountain into the Gale River Valley. In the far distance, a lone church spires dominates the landscape framed with white buildings. This is Franconia, one of the most picturesque towns in the White Mountains, set in a great basin with hills that sweep up to towering mountains, an amphitheater isolated from neighboring towns.

Franconia is bounded on the north by Bethlehem, on the east by Livermore, on the south by Lincoln and Easton, and on the west by Lisbon. In its area of 32,938 acres, it has a rich diversity: the wild and picturesque, the grand and sublime. Mountain streams in its eastern section unite to form Franconia Branch, a tributary of the East Branch of the Pemigewasset. In the western and northern parts of the town, the streams join to become the South Branch of the Ammonoosuc River. In the southern section, the Pemigewasset has its source. Lying within its borders are parts of Mount Lafayette, Mount Lincoln, Haystack Mountain, the Twin Mountains, and Cannon and Bald Mountains, Franconia Notch, Echo Lake, and the Old Man of the Mountain.

The town was granted in 1764 under its present name but because settlement did not occur, it was regranted in 1772 under the name of Morristown. Litigation concerning these two grants delayed settlement until 1774, when Capt. Artemas Knight and came to the valley. The town was finally incorporated in 1782 under the original name of Franconia. In the century that followed, tourists who came to stay in Franconia had a choice of many places, including the Sunset Hill House, the Forest Hills House, and Hotel Lookoff.

Guesthouses

Open year-round, the Franconia House was built *c.* 1878 on Main Street to accommodate 10 guests. At the end of the 19th century, the hotel advertised that "People desiring to visit the mountains forest and recreation for a few days or weeks during the summer months, would find The Franconia House a desirable place. The house is located a mile of the Franconia Inn and Forest Hills Hotel; a short distance of Sugar Hill, Sunset Hill House, Hotel Look-off, and six miles of the Profile House and the celebrate Flume, pool, and basin."

The Forest Hills Hotel and Cottages accommodated 125 guests during the season from July to October. In *The Grand Hotels of the White Mountains,* Bryant F. Tollis Jr. writes: "The Forest Hills Hotel, opened for the 1883 season, was one of the most beautiful sited and architecturally fetching hostelries built in the western sector of the mountains after 1880. Conceived by its first proprietors Harry W. Priest and James W. Dudley, it immediately caught on with the summer resort clientele." The 1902 *Tourists' Guide-Book for the State of New Hampshire* advertises: "Upon a sand hill, over 300 feet above the little village of Franconia, which is strung along the banks of that famous Mecca of trout seekers, Gale River, stands the Forest Hills Hotel. Four and a half miles distant are the noted resorts of Bethlehem, the Profile House, and Franconia Notch and Sugar Hill, while its nearest railroad

This 1880s view of Hotel Lookoff shows horse-drawn carriages filled with guests setting off for a daily excursion. South of the hotel is Ore Hill (1,980 feet), one of the sources of iron ore for the Franconia mining industry.

station, Littleton, is seven miles away. The hotel is environed by beautiful grounds and picturesque nooks, while the trails to the summits of nearby peaks are close at hand. Several artistic cottages grace the estate and in winter parties find the best of accommodations at 'The Lodge,' which is transformed for the occasion from a summer cottage to a winter retreat. The views from its piazzas are of the most majestic character; there are numerous drives and walks through the woods in its vicinity; and the air is a sure and quick cure for hay fever, etc., Music is provided during the summer season and the hotel has all the accessories of a first-class establishment."

The Forest Hills was purchased in 1902 by Herbert Hunt, who remodeled the main building, constructed a new cottage, laid out new croquet grounds, and changed the name to Hunt's Forest Hills Hotel. It remained in operation until 1954, when owner George W. Collier donated the establishment to the University of New Hampshire for use in the college's hotel management program. According to author Bryant F. Tollis Jr., "When this scheme proved unsuccessful, the entire property was sold to Franconia College, a two-year, coeducational, liberal arts institution that held title until it closed in 1978. In May of that

Shown are the Sunset Hill House (above), on Sugar Hill, and The Forest Hills Hotel (below).

Founded in 1884, Dow Academy, is pictured c. 1907. Lafayette Mountain is in the distance.

year the contents of the complex were sold at auction, and the main building sat vacant and derelict until the remaining shell was demolished for salvage in 1984."

Dow Academy

Founded in 1884, Dow Academy was the gift of Moses Arnold Dow, a native of Littleton. Desiring to honor Franconia, Dow presented the town with an excellent educational institution and paid the yearly expenses. At his death he left a large endowment enabling the school to continue educating the young people in the community.

Once the home of poet Robert Frost, this small white house on Ridge Road is now open to the public. Its porch offers a commanding view of Mount Lafayette.

The Robert Frost Home

Early in its history, Franconia attracted many summer visitors, especially those of letters. Among them were Nathaniel Hawthorne, John Greenleaf Whittier, Washington Irving, William Cullen Bryant, Henry Wadsworth Longfellow, Edmund Roth, Jacob Abbott, Annie Trumbull Slosson, and Lucy Larcon. One of Franconia's most distinguished poets, Robert Frost, lived here for from 1916 to 1963. It is said that he came here unheralded and walked about the country until he found a little farm he liked; he then approached the owner and bought the place—all in the course of an afternoon. The home commands a particularly good view of Lafayette Mountain, Frost's favorite. Frost was not known to be a particularly energetic man but rather led a quiet life, writing a lot of poetry, doing a little farming, and taking a small share in village affairs. His children went to Dow Academy.

Today the homestead is open to the public during the summer months as a museum, with a nature trail and bookstore. The small white house is located on the Ridge Road, which parallels the Easton road out of Franconia. About one mile out of the village, a bridge crosses to the western bank of the Ham River. The Frost home is a short distance to the left, on the right side of the road.

Of this iron furnaces built along the river in Franconia, Eva Stebbins Callender wrote: "built of granite stones, many being two feet or more in thickness and three feet in length, so strongly put together that but few stones have become dislodged. The stack is probably 40 feet in height, tapers slightly towards the top to support a large container into which the ore was dumped as taken from the mine. During the many years since the works were in operation, dirt and other foreign matter has found its way into the huge kettle and now quite sizable trees are found growing in it. Just back of the tower there are traces of the road down the embankment where the ore was hauled from Iron Mountain or Ore Hill as they called it then."

The Iron Industry

The original village lay in the Easton valley along the Ham River. The first mills, the first tavern, and the first of two foundries were located along the river. Iron ore discovered in the area led to the early growth of the town. Under the name of the New Hampshire Iron Factory Company, the industry flourished until the close of the Civil War. A deep belt of superb iron was found in Iron Mountain in 1790. The mountain shafts were worked by horsepower and man power. Two or three of huge dark openings remain along the side of the mountain from Sunset Hill at Sugar Hill. The Upper Works drew its copper from a mine on the slopes of Mount Kinsman. The Lower Works, which was built later, was called the New Hampshire Iron Foundry. During its heyday, the company employed up to 30 men and delivered 250 tons of pig iron and from 200 to 300 tons of bar iron annually, grossing a profit of $300,000.

A Reflection

For those traveling south from Littleton, Franconia—in the foothills of Mount Lafayette and Cannon Mountain—serves as the gateway to the White Mountains. As Thomas Starr King observed in *The White Mountains* (1866) "The Franconia Pass is not oppressive. . . . Everyone who has been driven into Franconia from Bethlehem or Littleton, and who has had the privilege of an outside seat on the stage, must have been struck with the gentle crescent line of the vast outworks of Mount Lafayette, suggesting the sweep of a tremendous amphitheatre, whose walls are alike with the ascending wilderness."

This picturesque view shows the village of Franconia with Sugar Hill in the background.

This c. 1912 view looks southeast along the Gale River into the village of Franconia, with Mount Lafayette beyond.

Ten
The Old Man of the Mountain

No other scenic feature of the White Mountains has been photographed as often as has the Old Man of the Mountain. Millions of travelers along Franconia Notch Parkway have gazed up at this remarkable resemblance of a human face, formed by the ledges on the upper cliffs of Cannon Mountain. The huge profile with all features delineated projects in bold outline against the sky, an accurately chiseled sculpture. The brow is massive and stern, as though stamped with the thought and wisdom of century. The nose is straight and finely cut. The lips are thin and parted, on the verge of uttering a thunderous speech. The chin is long and thrust well forward, betokening this hard and obstinate character who has faced with unmoving steadiness the storms of ages. The expression, although severe and melancholy from the ground, becomes amiable and pleasant when viewed from points farther up the ridge. The face, with its haggard and sunken cheeks, shows up best against the bright late afternoon sky.

The Old Man looks down the valley from a height of 1,400 feet above Profile Lake. The face is formed of five disconnected ledges of granite in separate vertical lines. The aggregate height of these ledges is between 36 and 40 feet (as measured by state officials in 1871). One rock forms the nose; another, the expression and upper lips; a third, the massive chin; a fourth, the forehead; a fifth, the eye socket. In 1859, one author inaccurately stated that "The Profile is formed by three separate and disconnected ledges covering a lateral distance of one-hundred feet. Of these, one forms the chin, another the nose and upper lip, the third the forehead. In height, the Profile is ninety feet from the bottom of the chin to the top of the forehead." Unfortunately, this statement was copied in many guide books and souvenir booklets for years afterward.

The Discovery

The person who knew the Old Man and its legacy best was Niels F. Nielsen Jr. of Plymouth. He told four possible stories about the discovery of his charge.

> First, According to Rev. Guy Roberts, "In 1805, Nathaniel Hall, then of Thornton . . . with others, was employed by Hon. Enoch Colby, who had been engaged by the State to lay out a road from Woodstock (then called Peeling) to Franconia. Late one day the party camped for the night at the southern end of the little lake at the foot of the mountain. In the morning, Hall, who had gone out early with a gun to hunt partridge for breakfast, happened to look up and see the stone face. He hurried back and brought his companions to see it. So far as known, this was the first time white men ever noticed it."

> Second, According to M.F. Sweetser, "The discovery of the Old Man was made in 1805 by Francis Whitcomb and Luke Brooks, who were working on the Notch road. Happening to go to Profile Lake (then known as Ferrin's Pond) to wash their hands, they spied the stone face. One said, 'That is Jefferson,' (who was then President)."
>
> Third, According to F.M. Kilbourne, "Dr. W.C. Prime, long resident of the Franconia region, says Franconia tradition among older residents credits the discovery to a Baptist minister from Lisbon who was traveling that way and stopped to talk to a man cutting bushes on a knoll by the lake and, glancing up, saw the face. The date and minister's name are not given."
>
> Fourth, according to Justus Conrad, "Some writers claim the Old Man was discovered long before the date given. The region was a favorite haunt of the Native Americans, and it is stated on reasonable authority that friends of John Stark made the first discovery while searching for him after his capture by the Indians."

It is interesting to note, however, that if a man named Ferrin owned the pond (second story), he must have been there at times before 1805 and it would seem that he might have noticed the face; also, John Stark (fourth story), captured in 1752, was taken north via the Oliverian Notch, not the Franconia Notch, but those seeking him would not know this and might have followed the Pemigewasset River up to its source in the lake.

Many other stories concerning the discovery of the Old Man exist. Undoubtedly, Native Americans spotted the formation much earlier, as they often camped beside waters, such as Profile Lake, where the fishing was excellent. According to legend, Native Americans worshipped the profile until, through the seer named Falling Mountain, they recognized it as a symbol of their doom, graven in the rocks of *waumbeket mechna,* the "White Mountains" of New Hampshire. To this day, the three symbols of the legend stand: the cannon, perfect in form and elevation, trained over the head of the Old Man of the Mountain; the face of the white man, gazing with calm, determined strength at the Native American; and the face of Indian Head, showing all the suffering of a vanishing race.

An Indian Prophecy

One August afternoon, a young chief appeared in the village and summoned all to follow him. He led his band to the brow of a hill, where a huge blue mountain shut out most of the sky. Then he spoke, saying, "It has been given to me by the Great Spirit . . . to know that very soon the side of that great hill will be torn in two." As he spoke, a loud rumble came from across the valley and, as it grew louder, a great scar on the blue slope widened and the mountain fell before their eyes. After the clamor ceased and the dust lifted to the sky, a great wound was left on the side of the mountain. The chief that night took his name from the avalanche: Falling Mountain.

On an autumn day seventy winters later, Falling Mountain wandered for the first time into Franconia Notch. On his way up the valley, he drank from a small pond and then glanced upward. Awestruck, he stepped backward. From the top of the sheer hill above, a gigantic face was peering out over the wilderness, a profile of mammoth proportions with an expression of serenity and patience. Through the evening and night, Falling Mountain stared at miraculous face, as if to fathom a great mystery. The next day, he walked down the valley to see what the face looked like from another angle. When he glanced back at the cliff, the face had disappeared. He quickly returned to the pond, where he was found by a scouting party two days later, still staring aloft at the great stone face. He told the braves to move the village to this place and, while they were gone, he walked up the valley and saw silhouetted against the sky an object, which he later called a finger, pointing to the profile. The village was established at the pond.

One day, a young brave named Bluejay rushed into the village, pointing to the southwest. "Another face, there! It looks like me, you, any of us," he told the tribe. Falling Mountain

The rough profile of the Old Man of the Mountain is silhouetted by the moon.

Profile Lake lies directly below the Old Man of the Mountain.

was disturbed. He had sometimes wondered why the profile of the rocks resembled the face of a creature different from himself and his tribe. The high forehead, the thin lips, the jutting chin—it was the face of a man but not of an Indian. The next morning, Falling Mountain and Bluejay set out toward the southwest. There, they saw the other face of rocks, a profile of an Indian, silhouetted on a ridge against the sky. The face was upturned with a look of appeal, distress, and agony. The trees above the forehead looked like the feathers of a headdress.

The pair returned to the village in silence. That night a bad storm arose. Falling Mountain watched as the great face, high up, remained untroubled by the storm's terrible thunder and lightning. One blinding flash shot a ball of fire straight out from the pointing object on the ridge, lighting up the whole notch. The chief cried out, realizing in that instant the meaning of the finger that spouted fire and of the strange face peering with relentless force toward the Indian profile. He called his people together and explained that the finger was a tool of destruction which, like the stone face above, signified tragedy for the terror-stricken Indian to the southwest. He said the Great Spirit had made both profiles and had written a prophecy in the rocks. The next day, Chief Falling Mountain gave the order to move, and the little band filed northward, perhaps as far as the banks of the St. Lawrence.

First Impressions

The existence of the Old Man is said to have been first made known to the world at large by Gen. Martin Field, who visited it in 1827. He sent a description of it to Prof. Benjamin Silliman, editor of the *American Journal of Science and Arts*, who published Field's letter in the journal in July 1828. As years passed, many people wrote their thoughts about the profile, including William Cullen Bryant, Henry Wadsworth Longfellow, Washington Irving, Ralph

Waldo Emerson, James Russell Lowell, Booth Tarkington, Anthony Trollope, Edward Everett Hale, Celia Thaxter, Harriet Martineau, and William Dean Howells.

In 1828, American landscape painter Thomas Cole ended up walking all the way from Franconia to the southern end of Franconia Notch, expecting all the while to be picked up by coach. Later, he described what he had seen on his walk: "There is nothing of the desolate grandeur of the other Notch. The elements do not seem to have chosen this for a battleground, and the hoar mountains do not appear wrinkled by recent convulsions. One of the two lakes, you here meet with, is presided over by the Old Man of the Mountain as the people here call it. The perfect repose of these waters, and the unbroken silence reigning through the whole region, made the scene peculiarly impressive and sublime. Indeed, there was an awfulness in the deep solitude, pent up within the great precipices, that was painful. Where there was a pleasure in the discovery, a childish fear came over me that drove me away, the bold and horrid features, that bent their severe expression upon me, were too dreadful to look upon in my loneliness; I could not feel happy in their communion, nor take them to my heart as my companions."

Nathaniel Hawthorne is believed to have seen the Old Man about four years after Cole did, although there is no permanent record of this fact, for many of his records were destroyed by his wife after his death. During his visit to the White Mountains in 1832, he quite likely went over to Franconia and sat by Profile Lake with notebook in hand and jotted the following: "It seemed as if an enormous giant, or Titan had sculptured his likeness on the Precipice. There was the broad arch of the forehead, a hundred feet in height, the nose, with its long bridge; and the vast lips, which, if they could have spoken, would have rolled their thunder accents from one end of the valley to the other."

"The Great Stone Face"

Hawthorne did not write his story "The Great Stone Face" until 1848. He submitted it to poet John Greenleaf Whittier, who loved the White Mountains and was at the time the editor of *The National Era.* Whittier paid Hawthorne $25 for the story and published it on January 24, 1850. In the story, three noted men were supposed to be the images of the great face: Gathergold, rich but miserly; Old Blood and Thunder, a famous soldier; and Old Stony Phiz, a great orator (supposedly Daniel Webster). When compared to the profile, they were seen to have a superficial resemblance but to lack its strength of character. In the end, the true prototype of the Old Man was found in a humble farmer who had gazed so often at the rugged profile that he had acquired both its features and its inspiration of calm wisdom.

In one of his poems, Whittier describes how:

Beyond them, like a sun-rimmed cloud
The great Notch mountains shone
Watched over by the solemn-browed
And awful face of stone.

Daniel Webster, himself, had something to say about the Old Man. Often misquoted, one version of what he said is "up in the mountains of New Hampshire, God Almighty had hung out a sign to show that there He makes men." Another version is "Up in the Franconia Mountains, God Almighty has hung out a sign to show that in New England He makes men." In 1851, a European writer said of the face, "It has not any nobility in its features, but resembles a very old man in a bad humor, and with a nightcap on his head, who is looking out from the mountain half-inquisitive." Bad humor or not, the Old Man's fame grew, people kept coming to see it and, in 1854, one year after the Profile House was established, the New Hampshire legislature made the Old Man the official state emblem.

Description

One of the best descriptions of the face is that given in William Oakes's *White Mountain Scenery:* "The expression is severe and somewhat melancholy, and although there is a little feebleness about the mouth, on the whole, the face of the 'Old Man of the Mountain' is set, and his countenance fixed and firm. He neither blinks at the near flashes of the lightning beneath his nose, nor flinches from the driving snow and sleet of the Franconia winter, which makes the very mercury of the thermometer shrink into the bulb and congeal. As you pass down the road, the Old Man's countenance first changes to that of a toothless old woman in a mob cap, and soon the lower part of the face becomes so distorted that the profile is lost. In going to the right, the nose and face become flattened, and at last the forehead only is seen."

Many illustrious people visited the Old Man: preacher Henry Ward Beecher, Chief Justices Charles Evans Hughes and Harlan F. Stone, naturalist Louis Agassiz, botanist William Oakes, and many presidents, including Andrew Jackson, Calvin Coolidge, Grover Cleveland, Franklin Pierce, and Ulysses S. Grant. Grant arrived on the scene in August 1869, a season of canoeing on Profile Lake, croquet on the hotel lawn, "ladies with dainty parasols, perching hats, leg o'mutton sleeves, wasp waists, and billowing skirts," and men with "top hats, morning coats and colored gloves," according to writer Ernest Poole. Recently inaugurated for his first term, Grant proceeded by carriage to view the Old Man and, according to a Concord newspaper, described the experience "as serene as though put on for that special occasion."

Preservation

Visiting the area above the head in 1872, some Appalachian Mountain Club members noticed the precarious position of the upper of the two ledges that form the forehead. Subsequently, an article appeared in a Boston newspaper stating that anyone wishing to see the Old Man of the Mountain should make haste as the face was in grave danger of falling into the valley below. The report disturbed Col. C.H. Greenleaf, an owner of the Profile House property, the location of the Old Man. Accompanied by a stone mason, a blacksmith, and others, Greenleaf made a trip to the Old Man's head to investigate the seriousness of the situation and determine what could be done to prevent a calamity. After his visit, Greenleaf reported that "the immensity in size and weight of the rocks convinced us that it was useless to try to preserve the Old Man of the Mountain."

In 1906, 34 years afterward, the Rev. Guy Roberts of Whitefield went up to observe and examine the head. He returned convinced that something could and must be done immediately. The 25-ton boulder, 19 feet long and 5 feet wide, that forms the larger part of the forehead was slowly being pushed off its ledge by winter snow and ice, freezings and thawings. Roberts remained devoted to his cause for nine years before finding and gaining the attention of Edward H. Geddes, manager of the Quincy Quarries in Massachusetts, in August 195. Geddes suggested a hinge solution using turnbuckles and half lewises to fasten the boulder to the ledge. The ice would still push the boulder out, but when it melted the hinge would pull the boulder back. Geddes made a brass-and-wood model and sent it to Roberts in March 1916. Roberts in turn wrote to Greenleaf, asking to meet with him: "Whitefield, June 17, 1916—The Quincy Quarry Manager to whom I referred has made a complete investigation as to much of the expense for securing that stone, has made a little brass and wood model showing just how it could be easily, safely, and effectively done, and has placed all this in my hands. . . . I would like to come to Profile as soon as possible and show you the model and talk the matter over with you." Shortly thereafter, the two men talked, agreed it was a feasible plan, and decided to go ahead with the work. Measurements had shown that the forehead boulder had only some four inches to move before it would be overbalanced.

The Old Man of the Mountain stares silently from the south end of Cannon Mountain.

The specifications of the plan are outlined in Mabelle Geddes Russell's book *The Old Man of the Mountain*: "The three turnbuckles, rods, and half lewises used in fastening the slipping boulders were manufactured by the O.V. Hooker & Co., St. Johnsbury, Vermont. They were made of Bessemer steel, weighing altogether about 450 pounds and measuring in length 3-feet 9-inches, 5-feet 6-inches, and 6-feet 3-inches, the variation in length being due to the distance of the forehead boulder from the parent rock. They were installed at a 45 degree angle due to the position of the forehead and the supporting ledge underneath the boulder." It took eight 12-hour days to complete the job. Before leaving, Geddes told Greenleaf and Roberts that, once a year, the Old Man should be examined and the turnbuckles should be painted to preserve and protect the steel from the weather. Greenleaf later wrote, "We were most fortunate in securing the services of Mr. Geddes, who was deeply interested, and expressed a willingness not only to place the turnbuckles in proper position but to do all the drilling necessary, and which must be perfectly done. A less courageous or unskilled man could not have completed the job."

The Guardian

The first time Niels F. Nielsen Jr. saw the Old Man was in 1947 while on a trip through Franconia Notch with his fiancée, Louise Colburn of Plymouth. After their marriage the following year, they resided for 10 years in New York. In 1958, they came back to New Hampshire with their four young sons and settled in Plymouth. In 1960, Nielson became an employee for the New Hampshire Public Works and Highway Department, first as a bridge construction foreman and later as a superintendent, responsible for maintaining and repairing many northern state-owned bridges. Not long afterward, he became a member of the crew dispatched to inspect and maintain the Old Man. He and the other crewmembers rode the tramway to the summit of Cannon Mountain and then hiked over to the top of the head to take strain tests on the turnbuckles.

Seeing the Old Man up close "was really exhilarating," Nielsen said. "I had sailed around the world several times as a Merchant Seaman, and I had never seen anything like him. My first impression was that he was one large, chiseled piece of rock, but when you get up there, it really is just a pile of rocks, a pile of rocks that should not be there at all." He added, "I don't believe anyone can be up there, even for one trip, and not . . . be awed at the . . . handiwork [that went into] taking a pile of rocks and shaping them into a great profile."

Maintenance

In December 1965, Nielsen assumed responsibility for taking care of the profile. His work was voluntary, but the state provided him with a crew and necessary resources. He and his assistants did stress tests on the turnbuckles and painted the steel members with asbestos fiber-filled paint, which insulated as well as preserved them. They also covered the cracks and canopies of wire and fiberglass cloth, recoating it four times with an epoxy mixture to prevent further debris and moisture from getting in. In some places, they shored up rocks and mortared them into place. They measured the position of each stone and placed checkpoints in the rocks at the top and on the face. To reach the front of the face, Nielsen descended in a boatswain's chair suspended by cables. He and his crew generally made as many as three trips each year: the first in June, to observe damage sustained over the winter months and to measure shifts in the position of rocks; the second in August, to carry out major maintenance and repair projects; the last in September, to make sure the cracks were dry and well covered before winter set in. This careful preservation work is sometimes undone by people who take the tramway to the top of the mountain, hike the mile to the profile, and decide they want souvenirs, according to Nielsen. They ignore the signs, pry loose rocks, and carve their initials in the canopies, letting moisture in. Some people even jump on the canopies and break through them.

During an annual inspection of the Old Man of the Mountain, caretaker Niels Nielsen (right) and Austin Macauley discover vandalism: initials carved in the protective fiberglass covering. Note the special turnbuckles that hold the boulders in place.

Niels Nielsen, caretaker, hangs in front of the nose of the Old Man of the Mountain.

Suspended in air, caretaker Niels Nielson and his daughter-in-law, Debbie Nielsen (right), inspect the Old Man of the Mountain as David Nielsen (standing) and others watch them carefully from the top of the profile.

Conversations

Nielsen said he had often felt the Old Man "shudder, sigh and groan" as the repair work was being done. He recalled one time when he was "1,400 feet above Profile Lake sitting suspended in a boatswain's chair, getting ready to drill a hole in the Old Man's nose and actually feeling bad about hurting him. 'Now, Old Man,' I said, 'If we are going to have a way of checking your face—it's sagging—I've got to do this,' [and the Old Man replied] 'Well, get it over with, you're making me feel like a porcupine.'" Another time, Nielsen went to work on the his left cheek, which had a hollow under the bottom rock. "I chinked the hollow with pieces of granite and mortared them in place, [and] 'Ah,' said the Old Man, 'that feels good! I was getting tired of keeping my cheek screwed up to them in place.'"

The Old Man owes its creation to nature and its preservation in great part to one family. Nielsen, guardian of the site for more than 30 years, vowed to continue until "the day when I can no longer step across a six-foot gap between two pointed rocks just above the Old Man. When I have to go around, that will be my last year." That year was 1992, and his son David Nielsen, who had been serving as a crew member since the age of 11, took over. David's wife, Deborah Nielsen, the only female who has ever gone over the edge of the Old Man of the Mountain, became his official assistant.

Bibliography

Among The Clouds, 1907, editorial, *Mount Washington,* Gorham, New Hampshire.
Anderson, John, and Morse Sterns, 1930, *The Book of the White Mountains,* New York.
Appalachia, Vol. XI, 1907, Boston.
Bean, Grace H., 1960, *The Town at the End of the Road (A History of Waterville Valley),* Canaan,New Hampshire.
Belcher, C. Francis, 1980, *Logging Railroads of the White Mountains,* Boston.
Belknap, Jeremy, 1862, *History of New Hampshire,* Dover, New Hampshire.
Bisbee, Ernest E., 1946, *The White Mountains Scrap Book,* Lancaster, New Hampshire.
Boston & Maine Railroad, 1902, *The White Mountains of New Hampshire,* Boston.
Brown, Martin A., 1946, *The Pycolog,* Concord, New Hampshire.
Browne G. Waldo, 1926, *The Franconian Gateway,* Manchester, New Hampshire.
Campbell, Gardner, 1938, *The Cannon Mountain Aerial Passenger Tramway,* Boston.
Child, Hamilton, 1886, *Gazetteer of Grafton County, New Hampshire, 1709–1886,* New York.
Chittenden, Alfred, 1904, *Report of the U.S. Department of Forests,* Concord, New Hampshire.
Colby, Solon B., 1975, *Colby's Indian History,* Exeter, New Hampshire.
Concord & Montreal Railroad, 1890, *Summer Outings in the Old Granite State,* Boston.
Daniel, Gene, and Jon Burroughs (Appalachian Mountain Club), *1998 White Mountain Guide,* 26th ed., Boston.
Drake, Samuel A., 1882, *The Heart of the White Mountains,* New York.
Early, Eleanor, 1935, *Behold the White Mountains,* Boston.
Goldthwait, R.P., 1940, *Geology of the Presidential Range,* Concord, New Hampshire.
Goodrich, A.L., 1916, *The Waterville Valley,* Concord, New Hampshire.
Gunthwaite Chapter, Daughters of the American Revolution, 1938, *Old Landmarks of Our Neighborhood,* Lisbon, New Hampshire.
Hanson, Dorothy M., *Bicentennial Commemorative Book of the Town of Lincoln, 1764–1964.*
Harrington, Karl, P., 1926, Walks and Climbs in the White Mountains, New Haven, Connecticut.
Hawthorne, Nathaniel, 1959, *The Great Stone Face,* Vermont.
Kilbourne, Frederick W., 1916, *Chronicles of the White Mountains,* Boston.
King, T. Starr, 1969, *The White Hills,* Boston.
McNair, Andrew H. 1949, *The Geology Story of Kinsman Notch & Lost River,* Concord, New Hampshire.
Metcalf, H.H., 1894, *Granite Monthly,* Vol. 13, Concord, New Hampshire.
Moses, George, 1895, *Henry's Town,* Concord, New Hampshire.
Mudge, John T.B., 1995, *The White Mountain—Names, Places & Legends,* 2nd ed., Etna, New Hampshire.
Musgrove, Richard W., 1904, *History of Bristol,* New Hampshire.
New Hampshire State Planning & Development Commission, 1963, *The Geology of New Hampshire,* Concord, New Hampshire.
Oakes, William, 1848 (1970), *Scenery of the White Mountains,* Somersworth, New Hampshire.
O'Kane, Walter C., 1925, *Trails and Summits of the White Mountains,* Boston.
Powers, C., 1889, *History of Coos County,* New York.
Proctor, Mary A., 1930, *History of Plymouth, New Hampshire,*
———, 1930, *The Indians of the Winnipesaukee & Pemigewasset Valley,* Franklin, New Hampshire.
Roberts, Rev., Guy, 1923, *Indian Head, Its Debut and Legends,* Whitefield, New Hampshire.
———, 1924, *The Flume, and All About It,* Whitefield, New Hampshire.
Rollins, Frank W., 1912, *Eleventh Report—The Society for the Protection of New Hampshire Forests,* Concord, New Hampshire.
———, 1902, *Tourists' Guide-Book for the State of New Hampshire,* Concord.
Russell, Mabelle G., 1959, *The Old Man of the Mountains,* Concord, Massachusetts.
Sanborn, Frank B., 1904, *New Hampshire—An Epitome of Popular Government,* New York.
Silver, Helenette, 1959, *New Hampshire Game & Furbearers—A History,* Concord, New Hampshire.
Society of the Protection of New Hampshire Forests, 1928, *Franconia Notch Dedication Addresses,* Concord, New Hampshire.
Spaulding, John H., 1998, *Historical Relics of the White Mountains.,* Littleton, New Hampshire.
———, 1998, *A Concise White Mountain Guide,* Littleton, New Hampshire.
State of New Hampshire, 1938, *New Hampshire, A Guide to the Granite State,* Boston.
Sweetser, M.F., 1876, *Osgood's White Mountains,* Boston.
———, 1907, *Chisholm's White Mountain Guide,* Portland, Maine.
Thomson, Betty F., 1958, *The Changing Face of New England,* New York.
Tollis, Jr., Bryant F., 1998, *The Grand Resort Hotels of the White Mountains,* Boston.
Ward, Julius H., 1893, *White Mountain Forest in Peril,* New York.
White Mountain Echo, 1953.
White Mountain National Forest's Waterville Unit Plan, The, 1978.
Will, Thomas, 1907, *Editorial,* Concord, New Hampshire.
Woodbury, Elmer E., *Historical Narrative of the "Lost River" & "Kinsman Notch,"* 4th ed.

Index